"If you've never traveled abroad (or out of your faith comfort zone), Mandy Hudson offers a front-row seat to the wonder, awkwardness, and humor of the global journey that stretched her own 'box.' *Coffee, Tea, and Holy Water* is an insightful delight—like an afternoon mocha frappe with a dear friend."
—Sheri Bertolini, author of *My Intentional Life*

"The Christianity that carries us into the future will be one that seeks to understand our brothers and sisters from all corners of the world, while constantly urging us to reexamine ourselves. With *Coffee, Tea, and Holy Water*, Mandy gives us an honest, humorous, and heartfelt account of someone trying to do just that."
—Seth Jones, Co-Founder of One Life International

"Mandy's travels will lead you from the remotest of villages to the most bustling of cities. Her ability to look at the world through the lens of faith and culture helps us better see Christ for who he truly is."
—Dr. Tim Harlow, Senior Pastor of Parkview Christian Church (Orland Park, IL) and author of *Life on Mission*

"With humor, candor, and Southern charm, Mandy takes her readers around the world (literally) in *Coffee, Tea, and Holy Water* and showcases with such thoughtfulness the beauty that exists in the diversity of God's kingdom and the value of connecting with the body of believers across the globe. If you've ever wondered if going on a mission trip might be for you, you should dive into the journey this book will take you on."
—Pete Wilson, Senior Pastor of CrossPoint Church (Nashville, TN) and author of *Plan B*

"It is both exhilarating and humbling to sit with other cultures and be exposed to their rhythms of life. With wit and charm Mandy is a prescient guide on an inspiring journey of faith and love."
—Jamie George, Pastor of The Journey Church (Franklin, TN) and author of *Love Well*

amanda hudson

coffee, tea, *and* holy water

one woman's journey to experience christianity around the globe

Abingdon Press
Nashville

Coffee, Tea, and Holy Water
One Woman's Journey to Experience Christianity Around the Globe

Library of Congress Cataloging-in-Publication Data has been requested.

ISBN 978-1-4267-9313-4

15 16 17 18 19 20 21 22 23 24—10 9 8 7 6 5 4 3 2 1

MANUFACTURED IN THE UNITED STATES OF AMERICA

To
Billie and Richard Bays
Bill and Nancy Rogers
Kathy and Tom McCarthy

Contents

introduction

few events in life prepare you for sitting in the backseat of a jeep with a bald, well-oiled Maasai tribeswoman.

I mean really, what can you say?

"Nice beads."

"I bet that haircut is really low maintenance."

"I like your legs. They're really shiny."

I looked at her, she looked at me, and the Tanzanian bush seemed to laugh at the awkwardness between us. I didn't speak Swahili, and she didn't speak English, so we sat in tentative silence, both of us thinking the same thing: *I wonder if we have* anything *in common?*

In a nutshell, that's what propelled me to make this trip—a visit to five countries to see exactly what I, a born-again American believer, have in common with brothers and sisters in Christ around the world.

How does the influence of spiritism affect the faithful in Brazil?

What is the number one question Britain would like to ask God?

What does Christianity look like in house-churches in Communist China?

How do people address God in prayer in Honduras? (*El Señor*)

And what exactly do Maasai women do after a discussion about God in their *boma*?

As it turns out, they go grocery shopping, much like housewives in the U.S.

My Maasai friend and I rode down the hill to the nearby weekly market where, spread out on thin sheets in the dirt, were piles of carrots, tomatoes, beans, and okra, punctuated by displays of jewelry and homemade rope stacked in tidy pyramids.

What does our heavenly community look like, with my Maasai friend and others I'll meet along the journey?

I pondered this while I awkwardly wove among the piles of produce. My mind was a mix of the heavenly and the mundane. *What is the best way to buy carrots? Do we know the same Jesus?* and *Exactly how many eggs do I need for a week if I buy them individually? Is her view of faith and of heaven the same one that I share?*

It wasn't a moment for *National Geographic*, but it wasn't your typical Sunday either. I began to see ordinary things from a new perspective.

Why does that matter?

For starters, it reminds us that we are all connected, despite the continental drift. It helps us put our needs in context and shows us how to fill the needs of others. And it reveals the depth of God's kingdom and his love for all of us.

And that, dear reader, was the entire point . . .

beyond the red sea

Perhaps you're wondering how I came to be sitting in a white jeep with a Maasai woman in the Tanzanian bush in the first place.

It all began with a cup of coffee. I used to work as a barista in a coffee shop, which gave me lots of time to think about coffee and one of my other passions—the church. At some point, amid making cinnamon cappuccinos and dark-roast lattes and coffee frappes and chai smoothies, I realized: The different blends of coffee are about as diverse as my customers. And I began to think: If Christianity is like coffee, the American choices are as vast as the selection in a five-star coffee shop. Some people know exactly what they want; some make it harder than it needs to be. Some want decaf so they can have the taste without the caffeine. Some just want the traditional, small, black cup of Joe.

It's all coffee, with one express purpose—caffeine. One beloved beverage that has been waking people up every morning for centuries.

I am addicted to coffee, and I may as well admit it. If you're thinking, "So what—a lot of people like coffee," let me tell you:

drinking two to three cups a day is not addicted. "Addicted" is carrying Folgers singles in your wallet just in case you end up where they don't have coffee and you need to heat water to make your own over an open flame. What can I say? I like having my own personal stash when I need it.

But as much as I love coffee, I love church more. I come from a state where you can't throw a rock without hitting a church. The church I grew up in in Alabama was one of five congregations within a 500-yard radius. The Christian culture pervades every nook and cranny—Christian bookstores in strip malls, Easter musicals in the spring, Vacation Bible School in the summer, harvest festivals (Halloween) in the fall, and Christmas programs in the winter. Million-dollar sanctuaries share neighborhoods with smaller ones sporting marquees with wisdom such as "Life is fragile, handle with prayer" and "God responds to knee-mail." Everything from pipe organs to praise bands awaits you inside. Church was as much a part of my upbringing as good food, football, or hot summers. It was just part of being Southern.

When I moved to Birmingham, Alabama, after college, I found myself swimming in the Red Sea—*red* as in, "a state that voted for George W. Bush" and *sea* as in, "washed in the blood of the lamb." I realized, if the U.S. is the most "Christian" nation in the world, I was living in the most conservatively Christian part of it: the Buckle of the Bible Belt.

From my earliest memory, church was a staple of the Sunday routine. Every Lord's Day you were dragged out of your pajamas and wrestled into church clothes. For girls, this almost always included a gigantic bow and frilly socks. Sunday typically included a family meal, sometimes at a restaurant, or sometimes just tuna fish and egg salad at your grandparents' house. On Sunday afternoon, everyone took a nap. At 5:00, we were chased into the car for evening services. Church wasn't some foreign ritual; it was simply a part of life.

My memories of church are scattered. I wish I could remember something holy to share with you from my wee years, but I only remember wanting to go to church in just my slip so I could be Smurfette. There was the time I was picked for having the "best smile" during Children's Bible Hour, where we watched puppet shows with angel and devil sock puppets. I remember getting prizes for bringing a visitor and being given ribbons for learning the books of the Bible and the twelve judges of Israel. Most fascinating to me, however, was the baptismal font at our church, which had a backdrop with trees like the Garden of Eden. I wondered how you could get a neat backdrop like that for your swimming pool.

As I grew older, I began to wonder about the "church" in other countries. Stereotypes, it seems, are formed at a very early age. When I was in the sixth grade, for example, our class had an "International Banquet." We had a week of geographically educational activities, including a detailed Parade of Nations with costume judges and a dinner featuring international cuisine. There were sombreros, chopsticks, kimonos, and corsets—yours truly representing Germany with an olive-colored beret with an orange pom-pom and similar-colored vest trimmed in orange bric-a-brac. I even had fake bread in a brown basket. We all looked like something out of a children's coloring book, to be honest. I remember watching our "parade" and wondering if people in Holland really wore wooden shoes and whether men in Australia really wrestled inflatable alligators.

How did this compare with what I saw in missionary newsletters—children with bare ribs and bloated bellies, veiled women covered head-to-toe in cloth, villagers who lived off of donated peanut butter and had to walk miles just to find clean water?

I began to wonder: *If being a Christian was such an integral part of my culture, what does* normal *Christianity look like in other countries? Not in the most extreme places on earth, but among everyday lives in other regions?* I couldn't help but contemplate what people might see on the frontlines of faith if they were dropped into a normal, medium-sized city in, say, Bolivia, Spain, or Egypt.

I was in my apartment at 5:00 a.m. a few years ago, attempting to get ready for work when the calling came. Coffee is a necessity at that hour, and my mind was blank as I wearily drained my half-empty coffee mug—the television droning in the background. Let me pause here to say that I am *not* an impulsive person. Those who know me will tell you that it takes me twenty minutes to pick out hair conditioner. But at that particular moment, the certainty that I was to travel around the world to write about Christianity strolled into my mind, fully formed and without a doubt. It was like immediately knowing the answer to a math problem you hadn't sat down to solve.

We can all debate how you hear the voice of the Lord, but I knew I had. I expected revelations like this to come with a little more pizzazz, but this one came with nothing but a cup of coffee.

After the idea sunk in, the question of what countries to visit arose. I didn't want anything extreme or too touristy—I wanted places that were different from the American South, but places where normal Christians lived. After a great deal of prayer, I settled on five random countries: Brazil, Wales (U.K.), Tanzania, China, and Honduras. With that decided, I set out to find host families and make all the arrangements.

Planning a trip to five countries wasn't easy, but thankfully, the Lord made it easier than it should have been. When I told family and friends of my mission, they offered to put me in touch with host families in those counties. I contacted those families, began raising support, and gradually plans fell into place. Plane tickets were bought at a discount, vaccinations received, and visas applied for. Nine months later, I was ready to go. Notwithstanding the major hurricane that slammed the American embassy where one of my visas was being processed, and the fact that the Brazilian embassy in Atlanta opened without the rubber stamps needed to process visas, everything went off without a hitch. In the end, I was very proud of my sore arms and my first plane ticket to Natal, Brazil.

coffee, tea, *and* holy water

Brazil

going to see the christ

If you are one of the millions of Americans addicted to coffee, you can thank a goat herder from Ethiopia named Kaldi. According to legend, Kaldi discovered coffee when he noticed that his goats became hyperactive after eating the berries from the coffee plant. He told the head of a nearby monastery, who found that a drink made with these magic beans kept him awake for long nights of prayer . . . which proves that coffee and church go back a lot farther than anyone guessed.

What does coffee have to do with the church around the world? More than you think, as I would soon find out.

Aside from an obsessive fondness for coffee, there are a few random things you should know about me:

1. I don't like tea, hot or cold. This may be anti-Southern, I know. But it's true.

2. I am deathly afraid of needles. Getting four shots in one day to bring my vaccinations up-to-date was quite an ordeal. And my second travel-related concern is being separated

from air-conditioning. I realize other travelers might be concerned with access to clean water, safe food, malaria, terrorism, or navigating the language barrier, but I turn into a female version of the Incredible Hulk in a humid, unventilated climate.

3. My favorite food is scrambled eggs.

4. If I could read one book of the Bible for the rest of my life, it would be Isaiah or Romans.

5. I think I might have been British in another life.

6. I love to travel.

When the day of my departure for Brazil finally arrives, I wake up feeling like Dorothy in *The Wizard of Oz*, when she links arms with her new friends and happily prances down the yellow brick road singing "We're Off to See the Wizard!" I'm really quite a serious person, but for some reason, the awesomeness of being able to zip across the world in a few hours has never worn off.

I arrive at the Miami airport, where literally every third person speaks Spanish. As the night wears on, the passengers crowding near the TAM airline gate all begin to look alike . . . Latin American. Finally, after everyone is boarded, I put on my eye mask and settle back for some sleep. The first thing I notice when the sun comes up is that the coffee is fantastic, meaning we must have officially entered the Brazilian atmosphere! I'm also excited because I have been looking forward to seeing Rio de Janeiro's famous statue of the Christ, the Corcovado's *Cristo Redentor*, my entire life, and today is my chance.

Outside the airport, a capable-looking driver pounces on my suitcase and deftly throws my luggage in the back of his black cab. Known as "The Marvelous City," Rio was the capital of Brazil until 1960, when the capital was moved to Brasilia. Rio is famous for its Ipanema and Copacabana beaches, its high crime rate, and its widely celebrated carnival season.

We drive in silence, though the presence of the rosary on the dashboard soon begins to make sense as the driver swerves wildly to avoid motorcycles and stopped vehicles. I compose a mental postcard: *Dear Mom and Dad, Sorry to disappoint everyone. I died in a taxi before I could see anything interesting.* Just then we pass something that temporarily distracts me from the fear of death. Out of nowhere are hundreds upon hundreds of dilapidated shacks on the hillside, leaning together, roofs tilted, like a rusty house of cards. *Such an eyesore on the skyline*, I muse, noting their graffiti. *I wonder why the city doesn't tear them down.*

Then I see washlines hung from the windows and realize with shock that people *live* in these shacks.

I soon learn that Rio is known for its *favelas*, or slums. They are named after the *faveleira*, a resilient plant that springs up wherever it finds root. Over a million people live in favelas, without sewage, running water, or electricity.

To my driver's credit, I arrive at the hotel in one piece. That afternoon, when the bus to the Corcovado arrives at the hotel, the tour guide looks at my ticket and says simply, "We are going to see the Christ."

Because the Catholic Church is based in Rome, Italy, not many people know that Brazil is actually the largest Catholic nation in the world. A Catholic priest first suggested a religious monument over the city of Rio in the 1850s. The idea was nearly forgotten when Brazil liberated from Portugal. A local Catholic association suggested it once more in 1921, and soon after, approval was given to construct the 700-ton statue on Corcovado Mountain, which officially opened to the public in 1931.

Our bus slowly makes its way to the Tijuca forest, stopping halfway up the mountain at a scenic overlook. There, perched calmly on the peak, is the 120-foot statue with his arms outstretched in the surrounding mist. The fog swirls around the mountain's tip, making him visible one moment and invisible the next. It is such a beautiful view, I feel I need to sit down and meditate, but the tour guide will have none of it, urging us to look down at the view of Rio: "Friend from America! (Translation: "Tourist with money.") Look this way! Friend from America! Do you see the stadium? Do you see our coffee trees?"

Back on the bus, we make the final climb to the top of the mountain, where freezing winds rudely greet us. I clutch the now-inadequate coat to my shivering body as the moist, icy wind solicits gasps from tourists caught in shorts and flip-flops.

Climbing up the long flight of steps, I can now see the statue's back. It feels kind of weird, like I'm sneaking up on Jesus. At a distance, he looks like he's ready to swan-dive off the mountain— but up close he is regal and slightly stern, with a tiny heart in the middle of his chest and his face solemn, as if to say, *It is a grim job, this business of looking out over humanity.*

The green islands below remind me of Neverland—palm trees with lush green foliage and deserted, misty beaches with cream-colored sand curve out of sight as they wind up rugged peninsulas. There are inlets and lagoons reflecting the mountains, as well as hotels and condos all sitting close to the water's edge. Opposite them, hillside *favelas* blur into orange and white, with the modern skyline looming behind them. It would be almost picturesque if not for the dreadful poverty they represent.

Rio is a mix of rich and poor, and I soak in the view, one of my favorite verses echoing in my head: "Come to me, all you who are struggling hard and carrying heavy loads, and I will give you rest. Put on my yoke, and learn from me. I'm gentle and humble. And you will find rest for yourselves."[1]

With the statue behind me, I close my eyes and set my heart free—free to blow around in the wind, tickle the face of the Christ, and dive toward the water in a rollicking swoop. Now that I am finally here, I wonder, *What should I do? Say a prayer? Make a wish?*

I look at the statue again, eyeing it carefully, as if it really were Jesus and I could ask him questions.

"Lord, there are so many things I don't understand. Why are you so hard to find?"

"Why do you seem to speak to some people and not others?"

"How much of my life is your will?"

I wait for something profound to happen, but I don't suppose God works that way.

My heart returns to me just as it left: in silence. It's as if the statue is trying to tell me, "Spiritual experiences are not up here. They're down there."

And the statue, of course, is right.

haven of grace

My stay in Rio is brief, as the next morning, the plane descends upon Natal (pop. 800,000), a city in the state of Rio de Norte in eastern Brazil. Bryan Carruth, the American pastor of a nondenominational church in Natal, will be my host for the first portion of my stay. Bryan meets me at the terminal, tall with blond hair, blue eyes, and a slight beard, looking more like a well-shaven Scandinavian Viking than a Brazilian minister. Originally from Texas, he has lived in Brazil for fourteen years with his wife and three sons.

Bryan asks if I am hungry. He explains that lunch is the largest meal of the day in Brazil, so we stop at a nearby restaurant serving local food, including the national specialty, *feljoada* (black-eyed peas). Brazil is also known for its amazing selection of juices. It is not uncommon to have guava, watermelon, pineapple, papaya, coconut, acerola, or cashew juice with the midday meal rather than soft drinks, Bryan says.

I eye him suspiciously. "Cashew juice?" *I wasn't born yesterday, you know.*

"The cashew is not just a nut—it's a fruit," Bryan explains. "Brazilians eat the fruit and send the nut overseas."

That would be just like Americans, I think. *Eat the nut; toss the fruit.*

While we eat, I ask Brian if there are any cultural taboos I should be aware of.

"Brazilians consider shorts kind of like we would consider pajama pants. They are considered casual wear, to be worn in your home," he says. "I should warn you that the OK sign is also offensive."

I try to get him to tell me precisely what it means, but he won't.

"Just use the thumbs up," he says.

As we drive to the Carruths' apartment, we pass statues of the three wise men from the Bible and the Christmas star, jutting in an arc over the roadway. *Natal* means *Christmas* in Portuguese, named because the town was founded on the Day of Epiphany in 1599. As we drive, I start to notice how many Brazilian houses are walled and gated with barbed wire at the top, kind of like mini-prisons. "Apartments are the way to live safely in Brazil," Bryan explains, "since the entry is controlled."

The Carruths' fifth-floor apartment is clean and well-ventilated, allowing the ocean breeze to flow through. It is pleasant, not like the heavy breezes of Florida. The window in the main living area boasts a splendid view of the Natal skyline, complete with a hammock.

The wooden-paneled walls and mango-colored bedsheets of the study where I am sleeping give the entire room an orangish glow, kind of like sleeping inside a melon, which definitely feels Brazilian. When I wake up the next morning, it takes my mind a full minute or two to process the fact that I am south of the equator for the first time in my life. Today is my first Sunday at Bryan's church, *Igreja Refugio da Graca*, or Haven of Grace Church. The church started about five years ago with 20 people and has grown to about 350. I am told that morning services don't do very well in Brazil; thus most of the area churches have one service, at night.

The church is in a converted office building, with the auditorium occupying the upstairs. Outside is an unfinished courtyard with bricks and rubble scattered amidst a fish-shaped baptismal. The inside is modern with plastic chairs, a video screen, and a plastic flame. On a tropical stand adorned with grapes and rose petals is the Lord's Supper, laid out like a work of art. A praise band and eight praise singers are to the right of the stage, including a young man playing the castanets. It is fairly easy to imagine the Holy Spirit flowing freely through the open windows on the steady, coastal breeze.

The congregation trickles in as the music begins. With the words to "Shout to the Lord" scrolling across the screen, a teenage girl in a yellow lyrical dance costume begins to dance, gracefully at first, then more enthusiastically. Then *more* enthusiastically . . . hair flashing around wildly. I, the foreigner, am the only one who seems to find this unusual—no one else bats an eyelash. Soon the girl is bending over, hair nearly touching the floor, then whipping upright, as if trying to give herself whiplash. I marvel at how she can do all this and stay on beat. Then I remember: these people are Brazilian—they come out of the womb salsa-ing to the rhythm of the contractions.

As I watch the uninhibited joy in her movements, I want to look away without knowing why. Maybe it feels too personal.

In the end, it is an exhausting performance. She looks tired. I feel tired. After worship, the lights dim for a video about evangelism in Brazil. Next is Communion, Catholic-style, with the congregation forming a single-file line and proceeding to the front of the church in unison. Communion is disrupted, however, when a chant from the back, "*Fome!*" ripples through the congregation. A group of teenagers dressed as doctors and lawyers stagger down the aisle, falling upon the altar—all part of a skit, as it turns out. "*Fome* means 'hungry' in Portuguese," someone later explains. "Why are these people hungry when they seem well-dressed and well-fed? They are hungry for Christ."

The chanting does not stop until some of the audience members are actually crying. Bryan then offers instructions to the congregation from the podium. They come forward one by one to share the Lord's Supper with the fallen members. Only then do the teenagers return to their seats.

Bryan then delivers the message—"Babylon Is Not Your Home," about how we should reject the culture of the age and how God has something better planned for his people in heaven. After the service, I am introduced to the family who will be hosting me for the night. The oldest teenager, Júlio, is the only one in his family who speaks English. He translates for all of us as the three kids and I cram into the backseat of the family car.

As we drive, I notice that almost all the suburban neighborhoods in Natal look like they are under construction, as zoning laws aren't as tight as they are in the U.S. Brazil doesn't have the system of available credit that the U.S. does, so people build onto their houses only as their cash allows. When we pull up to Júlio's house, a tin garage door slides back with a loud scrape, revealing a small driveway. By *small*, I mean Júlio's father actually has to bump the bumper of the second car to squeeze our vehicle in. Everything, it seems, is compact.

A gate with bars is unlocked in order to reach the front door. There is a lone overhead light in the main room, and the walls are sea green. All five family members share one bathroom. Brazilian houses have little carpet, no clothes dryers, and everything is open-air. Windows in the shower are at eye-level, which is a bit unnerving. Sometimes the showers are enclosed with clear glass, or are just a faucet mounted on the wall—no stall, no curtain. There is a small TV in each room, and both parents have laptops on the dining room table. With space at a premium, there isn't an absence of stuff . . . just unnecessary stuff. Even the walls are mostly bare.

I will sleep with Júlio's younger sister in a room with double beds, where, humming in all its glory in the corner, is a window air conditioner. The room is so small, it's like having an air conditioner in a large closet, but I don't care. I have never been so glad to see a thrumming window unit in my life.

Júlio looks puzzled at my immense gratitude. "We are from the south," he says simply. "We just have to have it."

Me too, Julio. Me too.

Natal's tropical climate varies only 15 degrees or so year round, with a high in the upper 80s. January is the "warmest" month, and July the "coldest," a concept I try and juggle in my head along with what else I learned so far—*lunch* instead of dinner, *apartments* instead of houses, *juice* instead of soda, *pants* instead of shorts, *Oi* instead of Hey, and the OK sign meaning . . . well, the opposite of OK.

What has made the biggest impression, however, is today's dancer. She was dancing. *In church.* Seems like that should break at least two commandments somewhere, but I'm not sure where. Back home, occasionally there will be lyrical dancing at a church, but it's choreographed to avoid any suggestiveness. This girl's dancing was not suggestive, and I finally realize it's not the theology that would have been out of place in an American church—it's the emotion.

With a flash of guilt, I realize I have just had the reaction of Michal, King David's wife, who looked upon her husband with disgust when he danced before the Lord in front of Israel after a victory. David's response? "I will celebrate before the LORD. I will become even more undignified than this, and I will be humiliated in my own eyes."[2]

I'm a little disappointed in myself. I've been in Brazil for forty-eight hours, and so far dancing in church is what sticks out in my American mind. And then I think: *If all it takes is a little dancing to stir my straight-laced Protestant comfort zone, maybe it needs to be stirred.*

city of the magi

After a few days, I become more acclimated to the Brazilian culture. Ethnically, Brazil is about half Caucasian, around 40 percent *Pardo* (Brazilian), and 10 percent or less African descent. Standard attire for the locals seems to be tank tops or shirts with pants and flip-flops. The customary greeting is a kiss on each cheek, followed by *Tudo bem?* ("Everything well?") or *Tudo bom?* ("Everything good?"). I am terrible at this greeting. Whichever phrase you are greeted with, you're expected to respond with the other phrase, and I keep forgetting whether I am the *bem* or the *bom*.

The most populous cities in Brazil are São Paulo and Rio de Janeiro, as the Amazon rain forest takes up most of the northwest part of the country. The population is unevenly distributed, with 80 percent of Brazilians living close to the eastern coastline.

One day Bryan takes me on an official tour of Natal (locally pronounced *Na-taw*). On the beach, he points out a fifteen-foot statue of the Goddess of the Sea, a lady in a blue gown with her arms outstretched. Her proportions are slightly distorted, with dark brown hair cascading down her back and a starfish dancing on her head. "The Goddess of the Sea is based on local mythology," Bryan tells me. "The locals bring gifts on a certain day each year to place in her hands."

"Why do they do that?"

He shrugs. "Good luck."

"Do they *really* believe it will bring them good luck?"

"Some really do," he says.

Casual as it sounds, this is my first introduction to the superstitious side of Brazil—a generic worshipfulness of anything deemed to have power over people, politics, or the elements.

Our next stop is *Forte dos Reis Magos*, or "Fort of the Magi." It is a quiet fort, but it represents a huge event, marking the first place the Portuguese set foot on the continent of South America in 1501. The fort is built in the shape of a star and strategically positioned where the Potengi River meets the Atlantic Ocean, making it defensible from both inland assaults and naval attacks.

Next we visit the downtown area. We pass vendors selling religious (and not-so-religious) relics in stalls—rosaries and pictures of the Catholic saints alongside voodoo dolls, pin cushions, and white-plaster models of body parts. Nearby is a blue, plastic bucket of holy water and several plaster objects sitting at the base of a historical statue.

"Was the person a saint?" I ask.

Bryan shakes his head. "Just someone from the history of Natal."

"I don't get it."

Bryan explains that many Brazilians revere the deceased spirits of those who had power while on earth. By the looks of the statue, which has been adorned with garlands, some people clearly believe putting a plaster elbow at the carved feet of a historical figure will cure their aching limbs. Two women approach the statue as we stand there. Dipping their hands in the bucket of holy water, one of the women makes the sign of the cross and they both pause reverently. I have trouble imagining someone doing this to a statue of Ben Franklin or Thomas Edison.

Our next stop is a "spiritist" store. Its right wall is covered with miniature statues—saints, John the Baptist, Jesus, Mary, and non-saints—all the way down to red-faced demons with horns. Tables and shelves are covered with items used in spiritist rituals: sticks of incense, candles of different shapes, vials of oils, clay pots, stones, wooden objects, spices, powders, baskets, and even plastic boats for sending offerings out to sea.

The stores are often used pharmacy-style by those who have gone to see a spiritist, Bryan tells me. The spiritist medium writes you a prescription for the objects needed to perform a specific rite. You go to the store to have the prescription "filled"—a certain number of colored stones, a specific type of candle. Bryan says such stores are fairly common—a similar store is just a few blocks away.

We then drive several streets over to a cemetery in the heart of Natal. I notice a variety of charms on the graves, which are mostly above ground—large, old-fashioned tombstones. Bryan points out what looks like litter on top of the graves—empty cups and bottles half-full with water. Locals place them here overnight, he says, believing that the "power" or "essence" of the dead person can rise up into the water and then be drunk. I'm not sure I believe him until I take a closer look at the plastic bottles and then observe several people milling around, "monitoring" their bottle collections. Bryan shows me the burial site of a mass murderer who was notorious for eluding Brazilian authorities before finally being caught. Even the criminal's grave is topped with a generous collection of bottles.

"Why would people want anything to do with the spirit of someone known to be wicked?" I ask.

"Power is power," Bryan says. "People want anything they think will give them an edge."

becoming a gospel

Speaking of power, I confess—sometimes I wish my story of coming to know the Lord was more dramatic. Instead, I think I am the only person I know who can claim to be sincerely, yet almost "accidentally," saved when I was nine. I remember it as clearly as I remember the olive-colored carpet in the sanctuary where we children were gathered for Vacation Bible School. One of the staff members gave a lesson and then led us in a closing prayer. He asked us to repeat his words in prayer to God if we really meant them.

"Dear Lord, we have all sinned and fallen short of your glory."

Sure, I thought.

"I realize that I have sinned, and I want to be forgiven of my sin."

OK, *who doesn't want God to forgive them of their sins?*

"I believe that Jesus Christ is your Son, and that he died on the cross for my sins, that I might be in heaven with you someday."

Yes, I thought. *All true.*

"I ask Jesus now to come into my heart and forgive me of my sins."

This sounded like a wonderful idea, so I repeated the words in my heart.

"In Jesus' name, I pray. Amen."

I opened my eyes, peaceful and content. It all seemed so obvious to me. *Why wouldn't you* want *to pray that prayer?*

The worship leaders then told us that if we had said that prayer, we had just accepted Jesus into our heart and should tell one of the Sunday school teachers after class. Instantly my stomach dropped and I began to panic. I was a shy kid, and I decided I was *not* telling a teacher. In fact, it took me another five years just to muster up the courage to be baptized.

I realize skeptics could argue that I was tricked, that Vacation Bible School brainwashes little kids, et cetera. But the sincerity of that decision is one of the most concrete things about me. To this day, it sits like a rock in my soul.

Spiritually, I've known frustration, confusion, contentment, passion, apathy, and a score of other feelings since then. But in the end, my decision to serve God permeates every cell of my being. It was so natural for me, like one day *realizing* that you love your mother and getting up in front of people to declare it. Still, there was an utter lack of sensationalism in the whole affair—no supernatural signs, no rehab experience, no mountaintop high.

Compare my testimony to that of Estevan, a Haven of Grace member who was a self-professed "intellectual spiritist" before becoming a Christian. In general, spiritists believe spirits exist and that humans can engage in communication with them through a medium and certain rituals.

A public prosecutor, Estevan joins Bryan and me in the food court of a local mall for lunch to share his story. He is an amiable thirty-four-year-old with black hair and glasses, looking a bit like a grown-up Harry Potter. Estevan says he was attracted to the rational elements of spiritism: its belief in reincarnation and the religion's charity outreaches. (Several prominent soup kitchens in Brazil, for example, are run by spiritist organizations.) While he says he later "fell in love" with the Bible, Estevan was still interested in spiritist issues and continued to dabble in it.

One day while reading a Bible in the study of his mother's house, Estevan came across a stack of spiritist magazines. "Lord, I know the Bible teaches one way," Estevan prayed, "and these magazines teach another way. I can't decide by myself. Please help me."

He reached out to touch one of the magazines, and at that moment, a violent wind blew through the room. Startled, Estevan put the magazine down, and it stopped. He touched the magazine again, and to his astonishment, the same thing happened.

"God, are you trying to tell me something?" he asked. He waited some time and touched the magazine yet again. The wind howled through the room.

"It was *amazing*," Estevan says. "I was shaken but very happy because God cared about me."

Still wary, Estevan asked a final time, "God, is this you?" For the fourth time, the wind howled decisively when he touched the magazine. He immediately decided to give his life fully to God.

Estevan recalls a later visit to a friend who had become a Satanist. "He literally looked like he was going to faint," he says with a grin. "He knew I had become a gospel!"

The words echo in my head: *He knew I had become a gospel.*

Estevan freely shares his story with others, but doesn't advocate asking God for signs when seeking the Lord. "He doesn't show himself to us all the time. It's not a duty he has to us, but he's there."

I learn that another young man at the church, Antônio, also has a miraculous testimony, which he tells me at a youth meeting the following day.

In broken English, Antônio says his life "began" at age three, the day his mother died. According to Antônio, he was in his mother's lap and she was singing. She told him to go to the other room, and when he came back, "she was crying and speaking very slowly." He realized she had been stabbed by his father, who was still holding the knife. It was a crime of jealousy, Antônio says. His father fled, leaving the boy with his mother's dead body.

"I was in the arms of another relative," he says, "when I looked out the window and saw a golden ladder descending from the sky and two people dressed in white clothes coming down the ladder. One of them took my mother's hand and helped her up the ladder into the sky."

From that time on, Antônio became interested in spiritual things. However, with a family history of spirit worship, that interest quickly turned to spiritism, not Christianity. Heartbroken, he often cried at night and frequently saw spirits and demons.

Ironically, Antônio's father—sentenced to jail for the death of his wife—came to the Lord in prison. Antônio remembers discussing religion briefly with his father at age eighteen: "I said to him, 'I see many things in the dark—why can't I see them in the light?'" Antônio says he started to read the Bible out of sheer curiosity—"just so I could know it was wrong."

One night while reading the Bible, the spirit of his dead grandfather came into the room. Antônio began to talk with him, as he often did with spirits. "I was so confused," he says, "but I saw in the Bible that Jesus' name was above every spirit. So I said, 'The name of Jesus has all power. Tell me who you are in the name of Jesus.'

"At that moment, his face . . . *changed*." Antônio claps both hands to his face and pulls them downward in a grotesque motion. "Like this." Then the familiar voice of his grandfather faded away and the figure's voice became loud and deep.

"I see that I cannot fool you anymore!" the voice said. "Then it started to choke me," Antônio says. "I cried, 'In the name of Jesus, *leave me*!' And he broke."

"Broke? You mean *exploded*?" I ask.

"Yes—*poof*!" He motions. "I knew this time that the Bible wasn't wrong. What was wrong was my life. After this, I started to search for God. "It was not easy," he adds, "because I still had nightmares."

One day Antônio saw a popular Brazilian evangelist, R. R. Suarez, on television and gave his life to Christ.

"God broke all the lies," he says.

When I tell him that many Christians in the U.S. don't believe in spirits, Antônio simply raises his eyebrows, then shrugs.

"What are some of the other things you saw while in spiritism?"

"Well, I saw Lucifer."

"*You saw the devil?*"

His eyes furrow. "Yes . . . Lucifer . . . Satan—how do you say in English?" He proceeds, saying that Satan himself came to his room one night during his search for God.

Surely this was the most grotesque vision of all. "What did he look like?" I ask.

He pauses. "He was very beautiful. He came to me dressed all in white, like a very beautiful man. He was dressed in a business suit." He mimics a man adjusting a tie. "He stood at the foot of my bed and asked, 'What do you want?' He asked, 'Do you want money? . . . Do you want to be liked? . . . Do you want women?'

"All the people who come to the dark come for power," he says.

At this point, Antônio abruptly stands up and moves his arms emphatically. "I told him I didn't want *anything* that came from him.

"I fell to my knees. It was really dark, but there was a little bit of light. I cried out to God—'Help me!' and I said to Lucifer, 'I don't want *anything* that comes from you!' He took one step back. Then another. Then, he broke—exploded into pieces. I started to cry."

I let Antônio recover before asking, "What are some of the other spiritual things you have seen?"

"I saw the Lord," he says, after considering the question. "I had a . . . how do you say . . ." He motions outward from his chest and up toward the sky.

"An out-of-body experience?" I ask.

"*Sí, sí!*" he says. "The Lord, he took me to heaven. In the center there was a large throne. I was . . . on my knees . . . crying . . . I could only see from the knees down," he says motioning. "His—

how do you say—*robe?*—spread out from the throne and covered everything. It was beautiful—all the light."

His eyes grow distant. "When he spoke, his voice was like many waters flowing together—like a storm. But it was good. And at the same time, it will give you fear."

"i see so many things in the dark.
why can't i see them in the light?"

After speaking with Estevan and Antônio, it is clear that I am not in Kansas anymore. My house has landed on a strange continent where people leave bottles on graves, talk with dead people and demons, and experience the Holy Spirit in a rushing wind.

I was skeptical at first. You may be too. However, in a country like Brazil that seems to have developed a spiritual "sixth sense," it stands to reason that sensitivity to the dark side of the supernatural would ultimately lead to heightened sensitivity to the light as well. After all, what Satan uses for evil, God uses for good.

For certain, the occult is alive in the U.S. too, but you have to leave mainstream society and go down a specific path to get into it. And that path often involves drugs and alcohol, making the testimonials of those who have left the occult suspect to conservative American ears. Not so in Brazil. Here, almost every congregation has members who have encountered spiritism, either personally or through a family member. Not only is spiritism part of the mainstream—enticing doctors, lawyers, housewives, and straight-A students—but also, because of the common practice of praying to the saints and other iconic personalities, many of Christians slip into spiritism without even realizing it.

As I talk with members of the church about exactly what it takes to spread Christianity, it is apparent that this history of spiritism continues to pose a major obstacle. And the blending of idol worship with prayer only makes things more confusing. It is not uncommon for a household to have more than a dozen statues—some Christian, some non-Christian—that the family prays to for healing and protection. When they think their faith has failed them, or feel they need more power, many migrate to spiritist beliefs.

Another hindrance is that many evangelical churches preach false teaching and extort money from their congregations. For example, one prominent church in Natal sells a special "Rose of Sharon" and encourages people to put it over the door of their home. When the petals fall off, supposedly the home will be "blessed." Another church has a special "prayer mat." Such practices not only corrupt the church but turn off nonbeliev-ers. Prosperity gospel teaching ("Come to God and you will be blessed") also poses a cultural stumbling block because of Brazil's widespread poverty. Attending church becomes another expres-sion of "What can God do for me?"

I decide to do more research on spiritism for myself. The "ra-tional," or organized, spiritism Estevan spoke of is a movement based on books written by French educator Allan Kardec in the

1800s. As proposed by Kardec, "spiritism" involves the study of communicating with the spiritual realm. Its key beliefs include: There is one "creator god." The universe is inhabited by spirits on other planets who live on a different spiritual plane than we do but who can communicate with the living. There are spirits inside humans, all of whom can gradually perfect themselves through a sort of "spirit evolution."

Kardec insists that spiritism is not witchcraft or Satanism. Still, there is no arguing that Kardec's theories heavily influenced darker offshoots of spiritism. Through the years, the term *spiritist* has generally become associated with those who would seek spirits for darker purposes. One popular strain, *umbanda*, is derived from African religions and is said to have originated in Rio de Janeiro in the early twentieth century.

Umbanda uses the spirits of the deceased to act as guides for the living and practices charity to aid in one's spiritual evolution and eventual reincarnation. It believes there are three general kinds of spirits—*pure spirits* (angels, prophets, and the Virgin Mary), *good spirits* (children, the spirits of those unjustly persecuted), and *dark spirits*. Unlike Kardec's spiritist practices, umbanda promotes the worship of spirits and certain rituals involving song, dance, food, tarot cards, and divination.

Quimbanda (also called *macumba*) is loosely regarded as the use of the spirit world to cause evil. While umbanda only involves "good" spirits in its teachings, quimbanda generally focuses on communication with darker spirits. It is separate, but closely related to another subsect of dark spiritism called *candomble*.

To help me understand some of the spiritist principles, Bryan introduces me to a retired couple at the church, Alberto and

Rebecca. Alberto is a former biochemist, and Rebecca taught at a local spiritist center for twenty-five years, as did her mother before her. Bryan translates as Rebecca spells out the practical levels of spiritism:

First is *mesa blanca*, or "white table" spiritism. This is mainly peace, love, and talking with the dead, she says. Then *umbanda*, which incorporates voodoo and rituals using the blood of animals. Participants might also be asked to ritualistically smoke cigars or drink a certain kind of alcohol.

Last is *quimbanda*. "By this time, the person is totally of the evil one and frequently possessed by demons," Rebecca says with a shiver. They use costumes and have certain tattoos, she says. They also drink blood and open graves in cemeteries, "but only the graves of those who are not Christians." I ask why not, but she just shakes her head. "They won't open *those* graves."

Quimbanda followers often grow their pinky nail long and use it to cut their flesh and drink blood. Sometimes they bleed so much that they need transfusions, she adds.

"How widespread are umbanda and quimbanda among Brazil's population?" I ask.

"It depends on the regions." Rebecca says São Paulo in the south and the nation's capital, Brasilia, have many adherents to umbanda, while the citizens of Rio de Janeiro tend toward quimbanda.

When Rebecca's mother later sought to convert to Christianity, she endured numerous spiritual attacks, including a confrontation with Rebecca's brother, where he painted the walls with blood. "He told my mother that she belonged to the devil, and he wouldn't let her change to Christianity," Rebecca says. Once Rebecca's mother became a Christian, she tried to locate many of those she had taught in the ways of spiritism and tell them about Christ.

At this point, Alberto recalls some of his encounters with spiritism, including one when their infant daughter couldn't sleep. Rebecca and Alberto took her to a spiritist, desperate for relief. The spiritist placed the baby on a table in the middle of a circle of twenty-four roses and then, as part of the ritual, made the roses levitate around the baby's body.

"*Levitate?*"

"Yes," Alberto says.

I search for the right words. "Didn't you think that was . . . *strange?!*"

He shrugs calmly. "I was expecting something strange. They only use good things [in their rituals] at first." *Like roses.* "They don't show themselves as they really are."

The signs and wonders are part of the allure, says Rebecca.

Rebecca, who has been a believer for eighteen years now, says her own conversion to Christianity was paved with great difficulty. Once, when praying for protection in Jesus' name, all the pictures in her house angled oddly at exactly the same time—something she blames on spirits. She recalls another time, when their seven-year-old son had fallen down a set of stairs. Fearful for his life, she called on Jesus' name, and precisely at that moment an ashtray beside her split in half, into two identical pieces.

When I consider Rebecca and Alberto's couple's testimony, I think back to the Idols R Us store Bryan and I visited and how strange this would all sound back home. But what Brazilians do with physical objects is really no different than what Americans do. Their idols just look different.

We are wrong to assume that simply because we may have more access to education or wealth, we have somehow evolved past subservience to "idols."

The dictionary defines an idol in two ways: "the worship of a physical object as god," or "immoderate attachment or devotion to something."[3] Brazil's stumbling point may be the first definition, but in America, we have more "immoderate attachment or devotion" to our lifestyles than any other country on earth. In other words, we've "progressed" from worshiping a block of wood, only to arrange our lives around other stuff.

Most of the world lives happily on one-fifth of what the average American has. The amount of time we spend acquiring, using, breaking, and buying more stuff boggles foreign minds just as much as believing that spirits attached to wooden carvings on one's mantle will give power or blessings boggles American minds.

The Bible is full of admonitions against idols, but they can pretty much be summed up in two statements from the Lord: "You shall have no other gods before me," and "You shall have no idols."

Well, I think to myself, *at least Brazil's idols actually look like ones.*

the north zone and lenningrad

Natal has its cultural quirks like any other city. Some are unique to Brazil; some are specific to the region of Rio de Norte, like the coffee—it is *sweet*, even when served black.

This confused me at first. How on earth could coffee get *so* sweet, like Coca-Cola? Was this some special bean? No, Bryan tells me, in Rio de Norte coffee is customarily brewed with a large amount of sugar. The locals don't understand why anyone would want it plain. By my second week, however, I am begging for bitter.

One evening, when I realize the housekeeper is preparing a pot for only me, I intercept her, enthusiastically thank her, and ask if she could please make it without the sugar. As Bryan predicted, she asks me to explain myself. I lamely tell her that it is customary in the U.S. to drink it plain. She then looks at me like I have asked her to do something shady.

Another of the things I will remember most about Natal is waking up in the wee hours of the morning to the hearty crow of a rooster. In the city. And a rooster without a good sense of timing at that. Dawn in Natal is at about 5:00 a.m., and this guy regularly woke up at 3:00 a.m. or earlier, crowing emphatically for two hours. I picture him perched on the window ledge above my head, like an Ambien commercial.

Overall, my visit to Brazil solidifies something I had always heard about Latin Americans, and other countries in general—that their hospitality is superior to ours. In the American South we pride ourselves on our hospitality, true. But Americans offer hospitality within limits, and often not until we feel we have the proper amenities. Would you invite a total stranger to stay in your house if it meant you had to give up your own bed and slaughter a goat?

In America—land of the free and home of the richest people on earth—hosting has somehow become a burden, not an honor. By nature, Brazilians seem to understand the importance of putting others first and offering hospitality despite the lack of perfect facilities. "Why is this?" I wonder. Perhaps other countries understand the imperfections of life a bit better?

I am still musing on hospitality the following day when Bryan introduces me to a young couple from the church, Gil and Teresa, who invite us to visit a poorer community on the outskirts of Natal called Lenningrad. Gil is one of several members of the church who visit the impoverished community biweekly.

As soon as we leave Natal, the roads turn to red dirt and the scene changes to something resembling a movie set—a Depression-like shantytown with piles of rubble, a few broken horse carts.

There are makeshift houses on one side, and modern rows of white, two-room houses, each with blue window and blue doors, on the other. Lenningrad is a Communist community, Gil explains, and is undergoing renovation. The new houses are free to residents.

Gil estimates there are as many as 650 families in the community. I ask what the parents do for work. Most of them pick through the nearby dump and then go into Natal to sell things, he says.

I then ask what seems to me to be an obvious question: "With modern Natal on your doorstep, why would anyone want to live this way?"

"It's their choice," Gil replies. "They want to live separately. The government has allowed them to move out here and leaves them alone." The kids can catch a nearby bus to school in Natal, he adds.

Speaking of kids, several children begin to emerge, barefoot and dusty, from the nearby houses. Once the children notice us visitors, they instantly swarm Gil.

One of the boys, Alex, is eager to tell us he that he had rocks in his stomach and prayed and was healed. He looks no older than eight or nine years old, so I am shocked to learn that he is in his early teens. Eight more children wander up, some of whom are Alex's new siblings. The mother says another woman asked if she would watch her children for two days while she went into Natal. It's been a month and the mother hasn't come back. "You are my children now," she told them.

We stay for about an hour. The sun is rapidly sinking behind the houses, so we have to cut our visit short. Pulling away from Lenningrad, Gil and Teresa suggest getting ice cream (which comes in flavors such as coconut, tapioca, and corn), but I only stare out the window—too many thoughts wandering through my head.

Why would anyone live like this with all the modernness of the city nearby? I wonder. Growing up in Lenningrad doesn't exactly prepare a person for college, but Natal has minimum-wage jobs that would at least get you out of extreme poverty.

"Don't they want out?" I ask Gil again.

He shrugs. "They chose this separation from the city."

I sigh, sinking back in the seat. You may as well ask why people do *anything*—why anyone would forsake a better way of life for one of constant struggle. Logic and stubbornness often get tangled, and logic doesn't always win out.

My good friend Lauren used to work with the homeless ministry in downtown Birmingham from time to time and she once asked a man on the streets why he chose to sleep under park benches when a free shelter was just down the block. The shelter had only a few rules—*Be off the street by 9:00 p.m.* and *No drugs or alcohol allowed.*

"In there, there's rules, but out here, there's freedom," he said, motioning to his surroundings proudly.

"You sleep outside in freezing temperatures, not knowing when you will find something to eat, and you risk getting stabbed in your sleep—and you think you're *free?*" I think to myself. And yet, how many of us do the same thing.

We say, "I don't want religion because that implies rules . . . at least out here I'm *free.*"

Then I wonder, *Does false freedom exist everywhere, even among those who consider themselves the most "free" in the world?*

It is a thought that needs to be finished with some ice cream.

the interior

because most of Brazil's population is fringed around the coast-line, a huge population gap exists between the coast and what is known as the "interior." In my final weekend in Brazil, Bryan arranges for me to spend the night at the home of a pastor/farmer in an ex-slave community in the interior called Capoeira, about forty-five minutes from Natal. To prepare for my visit, I talk with a church member named Donato, who spent most of his life in the interior.

"Men will kill people there for small reasons," he says.

Donato looks like someone you might meet in a Brazilian western. He was born on Red Sierra Farm in Campo Grande, and tells me he came from a family that was "poor in spirit, poor in money—dysfunctional."

"When I came to Natal for the first time in 2002, I had very malicious thoughts," he says. "I was trying to have a good life, but I couldn't seem to break through. I wanted more money."

"He brought a few friends from the interior to Natal to go into business with," Bryan interjects.

"I was going to get a gang together and steal cars and open a strip tease in the interior," Donato says plainly. "But when I got here, God changed my plans."

"I wound up getting a job from a friend, so I put the stealing on the backburner. But I still needed money faster."

The two men Donato recruited to help him steal cars died after being shot by the police. Soon afterward, Donato accepted an invitation to church—mainly in an attempt to hook up with a good-looking convenience store clerk who was a Christian, he says.

"When I got there, I noticed that Christians didn't carry any guns, so I thought, *I'll start stealing* their *cars!*" he says with a guilty grin.

The church service, however, brought a different kind of revelation.

"The pastor's sermon was about lost sheep. I thought, *I must be that lost sheep.*" Donato accepted Christ and started reading the Bible that next year.

In his view, sharing the word of God in its true form is the biggest need of the interior, Donator says: "Their greatest obstacle to receiving the gospel is idolatry—everything is a good-luck charm."

With Donato's words fresh in my mind, Bryan and I drive to Capoeira the next morning. One of the youth from the church, Milena, is coming with me to translate.

We pass white houses with burnt-orange roofs, swaying palm trees, and sticks in upright rows for fences. Finally, we pull up to the house of Elias, pastor of a local church, and his wife, Felice. To the right of their house is a pile of homemade bricks and several cattle pens beneath a shady canopy of palm fronds. It is such an unusual scene that my senses are confused. I can't decide if we are on a farm, in the desert, or at the beach.

The backyard is the washing area for both dishes and clothes. An outdoor sink is set up beside a large, orderly pile of roots— food for the animals. There are half a dozen cattle and one calf, a pen for chickens and roosters, and a separate one for goats.

Elias comes out of the house to welcome us in Portuguese. The house itself has light blue walls and a finger-painted welcome message on the wall written by the couple's daughter. A *Flintstones*-like bedsheet curtain separates the sitting area from the kitchen. Seated at their wooden kitchen table, Elias inquires of Bryan how his church is doing. We eat rice, tomatoes, black-eyed peas, and stewed chicken—the kind that looks like it was alive a few minutes ago.

After our meal, Bryan leaves, and Milena and I are asked if we would like to take a nap in a hammock. *Sure*, I never say no to a good nap in a hammock. Elias and Felice string one up outside on the wraparound porch for Milena and one inside the sitting area for me. Apparently there is a certain technique to sleeping on a hammock—known only to Brazilians and those who live in Margaritaville. After a few minutes of wrestling with my mine, I find myself eye-to-eye with my knees, bottom drooping to the floor. It seems the trick is not to sleep horizontally (which will fold you in half like a jackknife), but diagonally, giving your back support from the middle of the hammock.

After our siesta, Elias tells me a little about life in Capoeira. Despite its proximity to Natal, electricity only arrived in Capoeira in 1984. Most people do have a small television, but there is only one public phone and one house with a computer. The elementary school goes through the eighth grade. Elias and Felice attended school only through the fourth grade, but Elias continued studying, teaching himself to read.

Christianity came to Capoeira the same time as electricity, Elias says. Before that, there was nothing but spiritism. Elias remembers his mother taking him to a spiritist's house as a child; they said he had a calling and should work for them. Prior to his conversion, he witnessed the darkest versions of spiritism but won't talk about his experiences no matter how hard I beg.

"People who don't have God don't have protection," he says. "But God doesn't allow anything to happen to those who have intimacy with him."

Milena, Elias, and I sit down to a dinner of hot dogs, flattened tapioca patties, and mashed manioc root. Church afterward is in a pink building half a mile or so down the main road. The pulpit is draped with a white lace cloth, and the altar has bright orange and yellow flowers. Plastic chairs are arranged in a square with an open space in the center. There is no air-conditioning, but two fans mounted on the wall rotate calmly.

As I settle in an aisle seat, Elias is suddenly at my right shoulder, his face inches from mine. "What do you do?" he asks earnestly. "Do you preach? Do you sing?"

"Milena, please tell him I don't preach or sing," I say, trying to squelch the uneasy feeling in my stomach.

Elias considers this. "Do you pray?" he asks, forehead creasing. "Do you dance? Do you play an instrument?" Apparently they

40

take the Bible's admonitions about using your spiritual gifts in worship very seriously.

I ask Milena to tell him that I just want to observe. Elias stands, looking down in disapproval. Thankfully, the service starts as one of the elders goes to the pulpit and announces, "Let us pray for one another." This is met with spontaneous shouts of "*Gloria a Deus!*" Then the members kneel, facing their chairs. As they pray out loud in unison, it sounds a little like someone turned on ten or twelve televisions at one time.

Elias sits in a chair in the front by the altar, facing the congregation. When called upon, the congregation is ready to share. One girl gets up spontaneously to sing, and two young men helpfully beat drums and bang a tambourine as background. Someone reads 1 Kings 3:16, the story of wise king Solomon and the two women fighting over a baby. Elias's brief sermon covers a myriad of subjects, including giving God your best.

After church, we walk back to Elias and Felice's house. Milena and I are in a room with double beds—clearly having displaced someone in the family. I fall asleep as soon as my head hits the pillow. Later, I wake up in need of the bathroom. The single, bare bulb that hangs from the ceiling is turned off, leaving everything a thick dark. I feel my way out of bed and stumble into my flip-flops. Finally I make my way into the kitchen, where there is the same utter darkness.

I can tell from the breeze swirling around me that the back door is open, although I have no idea which direction it is. The wall I was holding on to ends, and now I am really confused; it seems a little too breezy. I realize, in a panic, that I could be standing in the middle of the backyard for all I know—the house floor is dirt, and there is no threshold to indicate whether you are inside or outside.

I have never felt so disoriented in my life. I can see a Capoeira story in the making, one they'll talk about for years to come: *American gets lost on way to bathroom and winds up in pen with chickens.* Finally, I feel a shoulder-high wall and realize I have been *in* the bathroom feeling around *for* the bathroom. I suppose there is some deep metaphor here, but I am too tired to think about it.

It is a huge feeling of relief when I finally make it back to the correct bed and discover that it is empty.

the sound of the bride

When Bryan arrives the next morning to take us back to
Natal, Elias and Felice gather to see us off. Elias steps forward
and immediately begins apologizing.

"I'm sorry if anything offended you. It was unintentional, and
I apologize on behalf of myself and Felice," Bryan translates.
He goes on to list a string of inadequacies—everything from
the house to the food to the bed to their hospitality. Seeing my
confused face, Bryan hides a smile. "It's customary to apologize to
guests as they are leaving. You should probably apologize too."

Wanting to be grateful, I apologize for everything I can think
of until Bryan cuts me off.

"That's enough. That's fine."

As I pack that afternoon, I reflect on the past few weeks. Despite the beauty of the beaches and the amazing fruit and coffee,
I think the thing I will miss most about Brazil is the wind—the
stiff, strong breeze that seems to be a constant, even indoors:
*"God's Spirit blows wherever it wishes. You hear its sound, but you
don't know where it comes from or where it is going. It's the same*

with everyone who is born of the Spirit."[4] And then there are the testimonies I've heard: "*I assure you that we speak about what we know and testify about what we have seen, but you don't receive our testimony.*"[5]

On my final night in Brazil, Antônio and I are joining some of the young people from the church to visit a local house for recovering prostitutes. I've never sat in a room full of prostitutes before. After the service we arrive at a tall house with a concrete wall, making it look more like a compound than a house. Once inside the gate, the front door opens, and three young girls stick their heads out to inspect us. *Are these the children of the prostitutes?* I wonder.

More childlike faces appear in the window until suddenly there are a dozen or so girls who can't be more than twelve years old, standing on the porch, watching the carload of newcomers. Then my stomach drops.

These aren't the prostitutes' children. These *are* the prostitutes. As in, former *child* prostitutes.

The owner, Susana, a middle-aged woman with kind eyes and brown hair, shows us inside. Susana confirms my suspicions—the oldest girl at the house is only seventeen, and they range in age all the way down to one year old. I close my eyes. *Surely not . . .* Thankfully, she tells me the baby hasn't been abused. She was, however, neglected, addicted to drugs and had burn marks on her when they found her.

My mind is still reeling. I was somehow expecting—and I know this is stereotypical—older, hardened women, not these sweet, unassuming faces who look like they should be at a sleepover. If there are tragedies in their past, none are visible now.

Suddenly one of the girls shrieks, *"Un Americano!"* motioning to me and rushing to the back of the house. There is giggling and muffled whispers. When she returns, she grabs my arm and wheels me around, looking into my face before rushing off again. "They'll be talking about you for days," Susana says with a smile.

All of the girls in the house, she tells me, are from the Natal area. The police literally found them in the gutters and brought them in off the streets, in varying conditions. One girl had tuberculosis. One was pregnant. Several were on drugs. Some were illiterate. One girl had been stabbed by her mother when she was ten. By the grace of God, they are in a safe community of faith now.

When Susana's family adopts a girl, they get a document from the government to make it legal. The youngest, Zoe, had a harelip when she arrived, but she has since had a successful operation and is healing. Susana gets her out of her crib. Zoe rubs her eyes and smiles sleepily, unbothered by the ten strangers staring at her.

Susana then gives us a tour of the house. There are fifteen girls total, and they all share rooms, bunk-bed style. There is a large kitchen and washroom, with a daily chores list on the wall. Almost everything in the house is donated—whenever they need something, they just pray and fast. "God has always provided," she says.

Total transformation has occurred in the lives of the girls since coming to the house. Their individual stories are varied—the newest resident has only been there a few days. Two girls are sisters, with parents who were abusive. One of the girls used to look "like a man," in Susana's words, and another "threatened to hit people until she read the book of Proverbs where it says, 'My hands are to bless.'" Another is so excited about her faith that she has been instrumental in the conversion of two other neighborhood girls.

Before we leave, the girls want their picture taken with "the American." For the first time, I am embarrassed. These girls—who have overcome so much—want a photo with *me*? Not wanting to be rude, I pose for a picture, knowing this will probably mean more to me than it will to them.

The youth from the church then lead a prayer in Portuguese, and afterward we all gather in a circle as Antônio closes his eyes and begins strumming his guitar and singing thoughtfully. Halfway through the song, Zoe breaks free from Susana and toddles into the middle of the circle. Turning in clumsy circles, arms outstretched, she begins to "dance," moving her head from side to side in the simple, uninhibited way that only little children can.

The other girls will probably have scars, but Zoe is so young, she will never remember anything other than love, I think, as she has a dozen older sisters, as well as Susana, who dote on her endlessly. Her life might be normal. *Joyful* even.

I ask the name of the song Antônio is playing. "The Sound of the Bride," someone tells me. When I hear this, I know my Brazilian moment has come. I, an American, have no idea what the sound of the bride is . . . but I bet these girls know.

Watching Zoe dance to the final chords, my time in Brazil plays in my mind like a montage. I remember how easily shocked I was a few weeks ago by things the Brazilians consider normal: dancing in church, encounters with the devil, finding the Holy Spirit in the wind. Now, after all these things, very little will shock me. And I will never think of the wind the same way anymore either.

For the rest of my life, I will remember *the sound of the bride*, played by one who truly understands what it means to come out of the dark and into the light.

And the image of a little girl, dancing happily in the darkness.

Wales

land of the cymru

flying over the Atlantic Ocean the next day, I turn my attention to the next country on my journey—the U.K., or more specifically, Wales. As the plane approaches the runway, I can see a classic British trademark: houses squeezed together in long strips called "flats." Row upon row, hundreds upon hundreds. Just before touching down, we skim over a rolling green pasture with grazing sheep, so close it seems like we will land among them.

We land without decapitating any sheep, and I make my way through the Cardiff airport to where my hosts, David and Karen Morgan, are waiting. David is a retired businessman and Karen a former florist. David is a jolly Welshman with a sonorous laugh. Karen is a soft-spoken redhead who is pleasant-ness itself. Both are very involved in a local evangelism course called Alpha and a mission organization based out of Oxford called Viva.

Once in the car, we begin the two-hour drive to the Morgans' home in Swansea. The Morgans live in an area nicknamed Mumbles, due to two odd hill-shaped islands just off the coast of Swansea Bay. (*Mumbles* means "breasts," but David doesn't want to tell me this.) Of the U.K.'s four regions—England, Scotland, Wales and Northern Ireland—church attendance in Wales is the lowest. In fact, according to David, who is Baptist, at one point during the past ten years more Baptist churches were closing their doors in Wales than anywhere in Christendom.

National statistics are scarce, but according to one postmillennial survey, thirty-five million Britons claimed to be Christians, but only one million attended church regularly. The Alpha class the Morgans host in their lovely home is part of a nationwide movement sponsored by a London church to address the questions those disillusioned with the church might have about basics of the faith.

It is raining by the time we pull up to the Morgans' home—typical weather, I'm told, for Swansea, one of Britain's wettest cities. Exploring the town of Swansea the next day, I quickly discover that every delightful stereotype you have heard about the Welsh-English countryside is true. Church steeples and smokestacks, pastures with sheep, green hedges, gray brick walls covered with ivy, tea, streams and country roads, right down to the habit of posing questions in the form of a statement—"You're ready to go now? We'll come back after we've had a bite to eat?"—and putting the verb first in conversation ("Sitting there, I was, when a chap asked me how to catch a bus to London. Told him, I did, that you can't get there from here, but listen, did he?"). It feels as if Tolkien may round the corner with a pipe in his mouth at any moment.

While the official language in all the U.K. is English, the Welsh nationalist party—or "Plaid Cymru"—fights to preserve both the Welsh language and culture. As a result, street signs in both English and Welsh are mandatory, and Welsh classes are required in schools. Wales has an estimated population of three million, yet the Dickensian tradition of singular shops in the heart of any British town remains—a grocer, tea shop, bookstore, florist, bank, post office, et cetera.

Wales is perhaps most famous, however, for its dazzling coastal cliffs. By afternoon, the dreariness of the morning drizzle has burnt off, and the sun is shining brightly off the deep blue water, so David and I go for a walk along the cliffs. I ask him to tell me about the Welsh Revival of 1903. One of the leaders of the revival, Evan Roberts, was the Sunday school superintendent at a local Methodist church in Swansea. Noting the apathy among those in the Welsh countryside, he prayed for revival for more than a decade. A local evangelist named Seth Joshua was praying the same—and specifically, that God would raise up someone from the working class to spread the message. Roberts heard Joshua speak one night and was so inspired by the sermon that he shared the message with his hometown youth group: *Confess all known sin. Confront doubt. Be ready to obey the Holy Spirit immediately.* From this one sermon stemmed a national revival that spread from Wales to the surrounding regions.

The effect on the Welsh cultural landscape was dramatic, according to David. Churches were packed. Public shelters became empty as pubgoers sobered up. Debtors paid their bills. One of David's favorite stories is how the use of profanity in the coal mines decreased so sharply that the "pit ponies" that worked there became confused—the poor horses didn't recognize the commands without foul language!

The Welsh revival resulted in 100,000 to 150,000 new believers by the end of the year. Several missionary movements were birthed, most notably, sharing the gospel in India. As powerful as the revival was, however, church attendance in Wales began to dwindle again over the next fifty years until most country parishes barely saw numbers high enough to keep their doors open.

On Sunday morning, I attend services with David and Karen at a local church where David is a deacon. Located on a corner in downtown Mumbles, they tell me it is one of the largest churches in the area, with 120 members. The sanctuary is small, with blue carpet, wood paneling, simple stained glass, and massive organ pipes in the balcony. The Lord's Supper is covered by a dainty lace cloth, and the pulpit floor opens up to a baptismal, which is something I've never seen before.

The preacher opens the service with a children's lesson—questions kids have submitted to their pastor, including everyone's favorite, "Who's got the stinkiest feet that you know?" The sixty congregation members in attendance sing "Give Me Oil in My Lamp" before passing around a small velvet bag with handles for the offering. I try to focus on the sermon, but my attention keeps wandering to that floor beneath the pulpit. Images of the Charleston swimming pool scene in *It's a Wonderful Life* keep popping into my head. All in all, it is a quaint and simple service—kind of like what the church in the U.S. looked like before it got supersized.

At the Morgans' house afterward, Karen serves up lunch for several couples from the church, a sumptuous fare of chicken and beef, carrots, broccoli, potatoes, cranberry sauce, and Yorkshire pudding. After dinner she stands up, cocks her head pleasantly, and asks, "Cup of tea?"

This would turn out to be a popular question, because the British drink tea about as often as you or I drink . . . well, anything—at breakfast, mid-morning, after lunch, in the late afternoon, and after dinner. As someone who has never liked tea, I find the tradition hard to avoid. Drinking it once a day I can handle, but not three or four times. David and Karen, being the polite hosts they are, recognize this and offer me coffee, but the coffee is a sort of weak instant variety made with water from the kettle, and not much stronger than the tea.

"Think British . . . think British," I tell myself as I sip my tea slowly.

We head back to church that evening. This time, the service is attended by only thirty or so. Afterward, I am introduced to one of the deacons—Curtis—a good friend of the Morgans who politely asks how many members my church at home has.

"Six hundred," I say, somewhat hesitantly.

His eyes widen. "*Six hundred?*" He pauses as this sinks in. "How many ministers do you have for all those people?" he asks incredulously. He walks away, still muttering, "*Six* hundred . . . !"

The church I attended in Birmingham—Church of the Highlands—has six thousand members, but I can't bring myself to tell him this.

Britain is famous for its small country churches with steepled roofs and a cemetery beside them. I think of the old saying, "We mustn't let our churches become tombs," referring to members who sit in a pew each Sunday of their lives—christened, baptized, married, then buried—but who fail to take the gospel into the world.

The next evening is the first installment of David and Karen's home-led Alpha course. Alpha is a video and booklet-based lesson series designed to discuss the theology of Christianity in ten weekly sessions. It is immensely popular in the U.K., with advertisements on billboards and buses across the country. Alpha gives skeptics a safe environment to ask questions such as, *Was Jesus anything more than a great moral teacher? How do we know the Bible hasn't been changed over the years? Why should we believe that Satan exists?* and *How does God guide us today?*

I take a seat in the back of the room, waterlogged from my fourth tea. There are about eighteen people gathered in the Morgans' den, mostly church members and friends.

The question of this session is, "Who is Jesus?" *A broad enough topic*, I think.

Once David presents the outline and opens the floor for discussion, the questions come fast.

"Why do we have to pray through Jesus?"

"Is rejecting Jesus the same as rejecting God?"

"Why are there only four Gospels—who decided that?"

"If God provides for our needs, why are so many churches closing their doors?" a woman asks in a shaky voice.

"People don't get stirred or moved by the sermons anymore," answers another.

Lively discussion ensues, because everyone is concerned about declining church attendance in Wales. No one wants to discuss the actual lesson.

One woman wants to know why Christianity is exclusive. A variety of grievances against the church and childhood preachers are uttered. After answering some of the questions, David eventually tries to steer back to the outline. We watch a twenty-minute video covering some of the most basic questions about Jesus: *What did he say about himself? What evidence is there to support what he said? What proof is there that he even existed?*

Even after this presentation, no one wants to talk about Jesus; the group keeps returning to the problem of empty churches. My thoughts are swirling. Complaining about church attendance without clarifying exactly what one believes about God, Jesus as the Son of God, and the Bible as God's Word, doesn't make sense to me. But I am trying to be a fly on the wall, so I say nothing.

As I listen to the group attempt a theological discussion without really discussing anything theological, I try and pinpoint exactly what they're saying: "No one's coming to church anymore, so God must not be relevant anymore."

What's real is real whether churches are packed or not, I think. And it's spelled out on the paper in front of them—simple questions no one wants to address.

Then I realize: *Perhaps this is why Britain needs Alpha.*

After the class, the den looks slightly deflated. Cushions are astray on the floor, and the couches have bags under their eyes. David looks tired, so I don't ask him any questions. I tell Karen good night, declining another cup of tea.

As I review my notes, I find myself annoyed because we got off the lesson. Then it occurs to me . . . maybe that *was* the lesson. What I mean is, the conversation tonight was a microcosm of what is going on all across the country. While people might like to attribute their doubts to more intellectual motives, most people's objections to God aren't actually coming from answers to the Alpha questions—they're coming from a reaction to the church, which many see as a lifeless institution. Try to lead a group discussion through the basics of the Christian faith—*Who is the God of the Bible? Is the Bible real?*—and you may as well be herding cats.

This seems significant to me. If this is true, perhaps it is too great a leap to assume most of Britain has rejected God on academic or scientific grounds. But it means the questions Alpha is asking, which some may think are corny or cheesy, may indeed be the right ones.

At the end of the day, we all have to ask ourselves, "Do I believe in a God?" (You probably have to be willing to at least *entertain* the idea of a God to take an Alpha course.) Then, specifically, "Is this God the God of the Bible?" If the answer to either of these is no, the conversation may still be waiting to form. But if the answer is yes, I think seekers will be surprised at how quickly things begin to connect and fall into place.

viva

The sun is shining brightly on the Morgans' yard the next morning—a small greenhouse, a pond, and blue wooden shed. I walk with David to feed the fish while I admire such a proper British garden. It looks like something out of a Beatrix Potter story, as if Peter Rabbit might peek through the shrubs and ask for a carrot.

By midweek, my plans to keep stereotypes at arm's length have been obliterated by a rudimentary immersion into British English:

"You've been to the store? Did you fancy anything?"

"I've got it sorted now."

"Would you like to ring your mum?"

"He probably thinks I've gone off my head."

In the local vernacular, cookies are *biscuits*, and biscuits are *scones*; French fries are *chips*, and chips are *crisps*. The trunk of a car, I discovered, is the *boot*, and the hood is the *bonnet*. Parking lots are *car parks*, lines are *queues*, a sweater is a *jumper*, and pants are *trousers*. Don't tell anyone you like their "pants," Karen says, as *pants* means underwear, and they'll think you're being cheeky.

In the U.K., babies wear *nappies* (diapers) and use *dummies* (pac-ifiers). Hop on a scale and your weight will be measured in *stone* (or kilograms).

I knew I was in Britain when a red-cheeked staffer greeted me at the gates of Cardiff Castle with a cheerful, "*Hello*, love!"

I confess, I hadn't expected so many differences in the British-American vernacular. The two are just similar enough to make an American feel at home, only to be confused when someone starts talking about how many *quid* (British pounds) it takes to ride the *lorries* (buses).

This is sort of how I feel about the decline of church atten-dance in Britain: it's similar to the decline of Christianity in America, and yet . . . *different*. Christianity is still by far the most popular religion in Europe. In a postmillennial Gallup poll, which asked Europeans, "Does religion occupy an important place in your life?" Sweden, Denmark, Norway, and the Czech Republic were among the top countries answering *no* (ranging from 83 to 75 percent), with the U.K. not far behind at 71 percent.

Britain, along with most of Western Europe, has what scholars call a *postmodern* Christian culture, meaning that Christianity had its "peak" and has been declining for nearly a century. The exact reasons for the decline are debated. Some attribute it to science, pointing out that the more "educated" society is, the more skep-tical it becomes. Many blame the world wars or a "loss of inno-cence" in the mid-twentieth century. Some point a finger at moral relativism. Some say the church fulfilled a social need that isn't necessary anymore.

One of the great Christian apologists of the twentieth century came out of Britain, C. S. Lewis. Lewis is best known for writing

The Chronicles of Narnia and his philosophical defense of Christian doctrine, *Mere Christianity*. Many of Lewis's other works are famous too, specifically *The Screwtape Letters*, which contain some of the most profound words written about the Christian faith. While we consider the decline of the church in England a fairly recent thing—born after the technological era of men on the moon, Lewis saw it coming nearly seventy years ago, back in the day of radio and newspapers.

In *The Screwtape Letters*, Lewis took a time-out from theological debate to write about faith, oddly, from the perspective of a senior demon, Screwtape, who instructs a younger trainee, Wormwood, in how to prey on human weakness. "For a long time it will be quite impossible to remove spirituality from his life," advises Screwtape. "Very well then; we must corrupt it." He continues:

> If you can once get him to the point of thinking that, "religion is all very well up to a point," you can feel quite happy about his soul. A moderated religion is as good for us as no religion at all. . . . He must not be allowed to suspect that he is now, however slowly, heading right away from the sun on a line which will carry him into the cold and dark of utmost space.[6]

I am still pondering this the next day as we drive to Oxford, C. S. Lewis's old stomping grounds, to visit the Viva offices. Viva's mission is to find Christian charities that help children around the world and to connect and support those ministries.

Upon arrival, we are warmly welcomed by one of Viva's cofounders, Patrick McDonald, a young man in his early thirties with red hair and dark blue-gray eyes. Patrick is the kind of fellow you like instantly, with a genuine smile and an energetic personality.

While we wait on lunch to arrive, the conversation quickly turns to church growth in Britain. Patrick says that three hundred seems to be the magic number for growing congregations: "Churches who manage more than three hundred members are able to grow," he says, "and those with less eventually dwindle. The ones that do grow seem to be making use of the small-group system."

Nearly everywhere in Europe, worship space seems to be somewhat of a problem, he says. Most historical churches are hundreds of years old and, as such, were built for fewer than two hundred people. Contemporary venues such as office buildings or theaters don't do as well in Britain because tradition runs strong, he says, and "church" is expected to be in a formal setting.

"There's a massive drift away from church by age thirteen or fourteen," Patrick says, raking back his hair wearily. "You really have to catch the imagination and enthusiasm for church by seven or eight years old."

This drift is something Patrick himself knows all too well. Originally from Denmark, Patrick was raised in the Catholic Church. His mother was bipolar, his father died when Patrick was in his teens. No one in the church seemed to care, Patrick says, so as a result, he wound up thinking people were "terribly bad" and that the church was nothing but hypocrites. He eventually found himself sleeping on the streets at fifteen, smoking dope, and living in a "hippie commune."

By Divine Providence, Patrick met a former supreme court judge of Denmark who introduced him to the Bible. Patrick originally thought the Bible was "an elaborate fake," so he studied it for months, trying to prove it wrong. Instead, it wound up having the opposite effect. "I began to think, if this is true, there's a dramatic problem, because 99 percent of the world lives as though it doesn't exist," he says.

Patrick recalls praying to God for the first time on his knees in his bedroom. "There was this most awesome, peaceful encounter—a knowing in your soul. It wasn't a made-up experience . . . something *happened*," he says emphatically.

"I made a friend—it was a simple as that. He just happened to be the God of the universe."

Changed, but not fully convinced, Patrick set out the next day to hitchhike around Europe, "just to see if God would provide . . . and he *did*! I woke up each morning and would literally say, 'Which way, Sir?'

"It was *life* in 3-D and in color," he says dreamily. "Life that wasn't angry or afraid."

Patrick contacted the Youth With A Mission (YWAM) headquarters in Bolivia and later became a superintendent of a South American soup kitchen.

"That's where I started talking to God about Viva," he tells me. "I was very conscious of God's love for orphans. I began to realize how much God wants to reach these kids."

In the early 1990s, Patrick had a vision that inspired the founding of the Viva network.

"It was like a film in my head of a spinning globe, covered by dark clouds," he says. "One by one, underneath the clouds came pinpricks of light. They began to get stronger and connect to other grids of light. I knew the pricks of light were the church, and I set out to find this organization that would connect them. I couldn't believe that such an organization didn't already exist."

For four years Patrick traveled the world on his inheritance to research the situation. Viva was born shortly afterwards, in 1994.

According to Viva, of all children born in the world today, 80 percent live in developing countries—Asia, Africa, and Latin America. As Viva uncovered through its millennium research, the problems facing Third World children are vast—hunger, no access to education or healthcare, physical abuse, drug addiction, child prostitution, not to mention diseases such as malaria and AIDS.

Christians are involved in child welfare projects, states Patrick, but they represent only a tiny portion of the worldwide church. Estimates suggest that there are more than twenty-five thousand Christian-based charitable projects serving an excess of two million children. As many as two hundred million youth, however, are living on the streets. This begs the question: What is standing in the way of doing more?

According to Viva, the three problems of modern charities are (1) poor organization, (2) limited awareness of other local organizations, and (3) financial sustainability. Many times, organizations have "tunnel vision," Patrick explains. What seems like common sense—communicating with like-minded local charities—is actually a much-overlooked bureaucratic function. When Christians are not linked together, every new regional problem such as food shortage, disease, or resource scarcity has to be dealt with as if for the first time. Precious time and energy are wasted. But when linked, these organizations can share knowledge, such as how to run a soup kitchen or build a school.

The Morgans recall one of these success stories in Cape Town, South Africa, where five different charities were providing free meals for children on Tuesdays. Viva approached four of the charities to see if they would choose another day of the week. They agreed—it was no additional cost to them—and now, the children are getting five meals a week instead of just one.

On the drive home that afternoon, I think about the magnitude of what Patrick has suggested, of trying to link all Christian charities across the globe. I can't decide if this is crazy or brilliant.

Well, it's definitely brilliant, but brilliant in a crazy way.

Back at the Morgans' over nightly tea, I ask Karen about how she perceived God growing up in Britain. "Well, I always thought of God as . . . an uncle," she says thoughtfully. "I finally came to realize he was my Father."

I ponder these words as I trudge up the stairs. If Britain's God is a distant uncle, most Americans think of their God as . . . well, Santa Claus.

And the question remains: How could the most "Christian" country in the premodern world, Britain, lose its place in less than a century?

And what does this mean for us in the U.S. today?

the prosperity gospel and the problem with pain

According to Alpha, Britain's number one question for God is, "Why do bad things happen to good people?" C. S. Lewis famously called this "the problem of pain."[7] This brings me to a trend I've witnessed in both Brazil and now Wales—the growing belief that "God wants you to be happy, healthy, and blessed," otherwise known as the "prosperity gospel."

To be honest, I have mixed feelings about this way of thinking. It is rooted in good intention—to encourage faith and positivity, and has moved a lot of people out of defeatist thinking. But I can't help but feel that its original intent—to emphasize the graciousness of God—has morphed into a subliminal marketing scheme of sorts.

The prosperity gospel is right on the edge of being biblical, as there *are* a lot of verses about how God delights in blessing his people. The problem is that, somewhere along the way, living water got traded in for the Prayer of Jabez. This is a tricky topic to discuss, because many who embrace prosperity gospel don't even realize it.

I heard of one church that challenged members to tithe for one year and, at the end of the year, if they hadn't seen a return on their giving (significant financial gain), the church would refund their tithe. This is the sound of one hand clapping—on one hand, I applaud them for the kind of faith that gets people outside their comfort zone. But I wonder: when making pledges like these, do members give willingly and unequivocally, or because there is a fallback plan?

And the prosperity gospel isn't limited to finances. In his international bestseller, *The Purpose Driven Life*, Rick Warren writes: "Many Christians misinterpret Jesus' promise of abundant life to mean perfect health, a comfortable lifestyle, constant happiness, realization of your dreams, and instant relief from problems through faith and prayer. This self-absorbed perspective [mistakenly] treats God as a genie who exists to serve [us] in [our] selfish pursuit of personal fulfillment."[8]

The truth is, for every verse a person can put forth about God blessing the righteous, another verse warns that the Christian life will be hard. As believers, we are encouraged to have faith in God, to live boldly and to believe he is always there for us. But using blanket "prosperity promises" to declare what God wants in the life of any particular individual seems dangerous.

OK, maybe I'm being hard on this line of thought. But an unhealthy approach to God ("I'll obey, but I expect you to hold up your end by looking out for number one") intersects with one of humanity's most burning questions—the problem of pain.

This is important, because I am beginning to think that this "problem of pain" is what ultimately turns people away from God—not the intellectual argument for a supreme being. People may like to *pretend* that their motives are based on more scientific grounds, but what the average person is *really* concerned about on a daily basis is what God, if God does exist, can do for him or her.

Somewhere in the middle of all this, the prosperity gospel promises "Come to church and your life will get better." And it does . . . for a while. But when something bad inevitably happens, seekers find themselves disillusioned.

"I put in my time. Where was God when I had a crisis?"

"I prayed my wife would get better and she didn't!"

"My family is falling apart—where is God?"

Apologists like Lewis would tell us that God allows pain to exist as a necessity of a fallen world so that we have free choice. It seems unfair when such pain may be unprovoked or be the result of someone else's poor choices.

Perhaps one of the best nonreligious illustrations of the problem of pain is Lois Lowry's Newbury Award-winning book *The Giver.* In *The Giver*, the main character, twelve-year-old Jonas, lives in a safe, innocuous world of sameness. The town's children have their occupations and their mates chosen for them. There is no death, discomfort, fear, or anything to disturb a peaceful existence. These conditions are borne by one man, The Giver, who is responsible to pass them on to Jonas. As the new Giver, Jonas finds himself immersed in a world he has never known— the world before "sameness." It is a world of pain and disturbing truth, but also of passion, color, music, and love that were eliminated when safety became the order of the day.

As Jonas learns, when there is no environment for pain to flourish, there is also no place for some of the joyful experiences that make life worth living. In other words, pain gives a certain depth to life.

Comforting to me is the knowledge that God is certainly not oblivious to pain—the entire book of Job is devoted to it. Some scholars argue that the book of Job is one of the oldest books in the Bible, if not *the* oldest. It's as if God knew this was going to be important and wanted to be sure we had an example of how to deal with it. God ensures a profound, central example of the problem of pain.

It's interesting that the first thing Satan accuses Job of before the Lord is, in essence, a focus on prosperity gospel: "Does Job revere God for nothing? . . . Haven't you fenced him in—his house and all he has—and blessed the work of his hands so that his possessions extend throughout the earth? But stretch out your hand and strike all he has. He will certainly curse you to your face."[9] The book chronicles a conversation between Job and his friends after Job suffered tragedy after tragedy. After chapters and chapters of chatter and questioning (*What have I done wrong? Why did this happen? Is God angry with me?*), God slices through it all with one simple question: "Prepare yourself like a man; / I will interrogate you, and you will respond to me. / Where were you when I laid the earth's foundation?"[10]

The point is, God does not owe us individualized, detailed explanations for the pain in our lives. ("Would you question my justice, / deem me guilty so you can be innocent?"[11]) God's answer might seem humorous or severe, based on your perspective: "Can you send lightning so that it goes / and then says to you 'I'm here'? . . . Can you issue an order to the clouds? . . . Who gave birth to heaven's frost? . . . Have you surveyed the earth's expanses? / Tell me if you know everything about it."[12]

As a child, I thought God's reply to Job did not answer the question. As an adult, I realize fully that it does.

british tea and pumpkin pie

The town of Swansea is centered around Swansea Bay, a part of the Bristol Channel. Impressively, Swansea Bay has the second-largest tidal recession in the world, meaning that when the tide is in at night, the bay looks normal, but when it is out during the day, the town appears curved around a strange, muddy quagmire.

On Sunday morning I visit a Welsh-speaking church with Karen. The first thing I notice is that the church is sitting smack in the middle of a graveyard . . . no joke. Entering the iron gates, we pass the massive tombstones in the front yard, some tall and slender, some sculpted and wide. Attendance seems to be getting poorer the more churches I visit, and I am starting to believe David and Karen when they say theirs is one of the largest in Wales. This time there are only forty in attendance—thirty-five women and five men in a sanctuary that could easily hold two-hundred-fifty people. To add to the starkness, everyone is sitting in the back five rows.

The minister looks to be in his forties and, aside from me, is probably the youngest person in the room, which makes the service look more like a poorly attended senior-citizen gathering than anything else. The minister says a Welsh prayer and an English prayer, which goes on for at least twenty minutes. I crack my eyes to see if any of the white-haired little old ladies are nodding off. It's hard to tell, but we move on to the offertory, passing a wooden box on a stick with handles on each side, kind of like a miniature coffin. Once the offering is resting in peace, we proceed to the sermon, "God Is Love," which is also in Welsh. I sit there trying to imagine what the church might have looked like when it was full, and I wonder: *Why have a church service in a dying language? Why keep a church open for forty people?*

To be fair, not all churches in Wales are like this one—some, like the Morgans' church, are trying hard to grow. But this particular church illustrates a stark reality and asks important questions: Is *church* about advancing the gospel? The comfort of tradition? *Is it about those on the inside or those on the outside?*

I realize that congregations in the U.S. sometimes fail to ask these questions too. This Welsh church just offers an exaggerated picture of what the services will eventually look like if we don't ask them.

After the service, I join Curtis and his wife for lunch—a roast with vegetables, cabbage, potatoes . . . and tea, of course. Tea is now offered to visitors at any time of day, but it was traditionally served after the main meal of the day—thus the custom of mid-afternoon tea. The choices are to have a *normal tea* (with cookies), a *cream tea* (accompanied by cream-filled pastries or cakes) or *high tea*, where sandwiches and appetizers are served in place of the evening meal.

For the evening service we visit a church where Curtis is guest preaching. This time, there are only fifteen or twenty in attendance. We then meet David and Karen back at their church, where the ladies present me with a large, misshapen pumpkin and ask me to make them a pumpkin pie for the next Alpha class. I try to explain that in the U.S. we use canned pumpkin and that it would be an oddity to use *real* pumpkin, but they don't believe me.

They all gasp when I tell them pumpkin pie is served with ice cream—including Karen, who thought it was an entrée like squash. I now feel compelled to prove that Americans aren't crazy for liking a dessert made out of a large gourd. Still, I try again to convince them that the pie will taste better with canned pumpkin, but they don't sell it in Britain, and they all want the prize pumpkin to become the American dish they've heard so much about.

I worry about the pumpkin the entire car ride home. It sits in the seat across from me like an underage passenger. Never underestimate the power of a Welsh cook like Karen, however. By the next morning, she has somehow found instructions on how to cook a pumpkin (scoop out the seeds, cube, boil, and mash it, in case you were wondering).

"Why don't we make pumpkin soup to go along with it for dinner?" she suggests cheerfully.

Well, there's no going back now.

One of Swansea's most famous natives was the poet Dylan Thomas. Born in 1914, Thomas is immortalized by a statue in the town's harbor. He lived a relatively short life, passing away at age thirty-nine, but not before penning one of his most famous works, "Do Not Go Gentle into That Good Night":

Do not go gentle into that good night . . .

Rage, rage against the dying of the light.[13]

The next morning, I take a walk around Swansea harbor, past the statue, and on to Mumbles Castle, which sits innocently on a hill overlooking the town. I join David and Karen for an afternoon stroll along the Gowers, one of Wales's most famous stretches of coastline. Both the sky and the water are a brilliant light blue. It is a distinctly British scene—rolling countryside, rugged cliffs, horse and hound.

As we walk, I think of the small country churches and the white-haired Welsh church service and wonder if America, "one nation under God," will become like Great Britain. Maybe? A short time in Wales doesn't make me an expert, but I can offer a few thoughts.

It seems that Britain has succumbed to a state of indifference about God. Most Americans do seem to believe on some level— they just let their faith get choked out by lifestyle.

In Britain, what its people see as hundreds of years of stuffy tradition has evolved relatively little, and people have become disenchanted with the church. The American church isn't that old; nonbelievers are usually disenchanted with the actual members of the church, whom they perceive as hypocrites.

One noticeable difference I see in the two cultures is that Americans are more likely to modify the church to fit the culture, which can be both good and bad. In other words, America might wind up where Britain is, but by a slightly different path.

Contemporary author Francis Chan sums it up in a pretty profound statement:

> We need to stop giving people excuses not to believe in God. You've probably heard the expression, *I believe in God, just not organized religion.* I don't think people would say that if the church truly lived like we are called to live. The expression would change to *I can't deny what the church does, but I don't believe in their God.* At least then they'd address their rejection of God rather than use the church as a scapegoat.[14]

I'm still thinking about this as David, Karen, and I carry the pies and the homemade pumpkin soup to the Alpha meeting that night. As we sit there with our dessert and tea, I keep trying to put my finger on the reason for Britain's turn from Christianity and I keep coming up with . . . *nothing.*

And maybe that's the entire point. After all, the act of wandering from faith isn't always a freefall into hedonism—sometimes it is a slow, apathetic slide, unmarked by anything obvious on the exterior. To quote a letter from Screwtape to Wormwood:

> It's funny how mortals always picture us as putting things into their minds: in reality, our best work is done by keeping things out. . . . Do remember, the only thing that matters is the extent to which you separate the man from the Enemy. It does not matter how small the sins are provided that their cumulative effect is to edge the man away from the Light and out into the Nothing. . . . Indeed, the safest road to Hell is the gradual one—the gentle slope, soft underfoot, without sudden turnings, without milestones, without signposts.[15]

feed the birds

The next day I say farewell to Swansea, boarding a train that will take me to London for a few days of sightseeing. I settle in with a guidebook as the drizzling, green countryside flashes past the window. I soon learn that Christianity in England has a storied history involving an awful lot of royals named Edward, Henry, and John. I immerse myself in everything from the Crusades to the Magna Carta to the founding of the Church of England. Before I know it, the train is pulling up to Paddington Station in London. I haul my luggage through the streets to a bed and breakfast inn. First stop: Westminster Abbey.

A sign outside the abbey kindly warns that there is a history of pickpockets in the area. Thus, craning your head upwards at the magnificent set of twin Gothic towers is best done with one hand on your personal belongings at all times.

The history of Westminster dates back to before the actual cathedral was even built. According to tradition, a religious shrine was first built on the site after a local fisherman reportedly saw a vision of Saint Peter. The abbey was constructed by Edward the

Confessor to house monks, and eventually rebuilt, over a period of three hundred years, in the elegant Gothic style it boasts today.

All English monarchs since William the Conqueror (1066) have been crowned in the abbey, except those who had no coronations: Edward V, Edward VIII, and Lady Jane Grey. Westminster is the official site for other royal occasions such as burials and certain weddings, including that of Prince William and Catherine.

As I enter the church, one thing seems sure: Westminster Abbey is getting pretty crowded with dead people. With regard to the metaphor of not letting our churches become tombs, I feel that we may have progressed a little too far in the wrong direction—now the tombs are actually *inside* the church. Members of the royal family were buried within the walls almost exclusively up until 1560, but since then the restrictions have been loosened to include approximately 3,500 souls buried on the grounds.

Understandably, I suppose, Westminster is a Who's Who graveyard for the nation of Great Britain. Aside from monarchs, famous statesmen, and game-changers such as Isaac Newton, William Wilberforce, and Charles Darwin are buried here. Literary greats such as Browning, Chaucer, Dickens, Kipling, and Tennyson are in a part of the South Transept called "Poet's Corner." There are additional monuments to Shakespeare, Jane Austen, Lord Byron, Winston Churchill, Sir Francis Drake, Oscar Wilde, and Henry Wadsworth Longfellow.

The next day I take one of the red double-decker bus tours of London and arrive at Buckingham Palace for the changing of the guard ceremony. The crowd is packed so tight with people that one can hardly move. The ceremony is preceded by a parade of bobbies in red coats on horseback. Inside the gates they pace up and down a black strip of carpet, the band playing upbeat, if not surprising music like "Get Down Tonight" and "Eye of the Tiger."

The nearby London Museum has a short film dedicated to the Great Fire of London, which burned through the medieval city for three days in September of 1666 and destroyed a whopping 80 percent of it. The blaze is said to have started at a bakery on Pudding Lane, consuming the congestion of wooden houses and thatched straw roofs until an estimated 70,000 of the city's 80,000 were homeless.

A trip to London wouldn't be complete, however, without a visit to historical St. Paul's Cathedral. The St. Paul's of modern times is actually the fifth St. Paul's constructed on the spot. It was created in 604, but burned down in 675. The cathedral was pillaged by Vikings in 961, burnt down again in 1087, struck by lightning in the 1500s and finally, almost totally charred by London's Great Fire. The current St. Paul's is nearly hidden in the city's financial district—modern London has grown up around it and now threatens to squash it. The building was completed in a youthful 1708, withstanding targeted World War II bombing blitzes in both October 1940 and April 1941.

When I think of St. Paul's, I can't help but think of the "Feed the Birds" scene in a favorite childhood movie, *Mary Poppins*. Young Michael is given tuppence and wants to use it to buy food for the birds on the steps of St. Paul's. His father, a banker, will have none of it, wanting the lad to invest his money instead.

There is no modern birdwoman on the steps of St. Paul's to give your money to today, but I am delighted to learn that "tuppence" and the birds of St. Paul's are not a myth. In fact, I might be the only one on this fine afternoon who is enamored with the birds—they annoy everyone else.

The interior dome of St. Paul's is brilliant but dizzying, as I'm not used to looking up fifteen stories at curved architecture. Like Westminster, St. Paul's also has a crypt in the basement, home to more than two hundred memorials. Notable funerals it has hosted include those of Lord Nelson, the Duke of Wellington, and Winston Churchill.

One of the most spectacular things about St. Paul's, however, is the view from the top. The cathedral offers a view of the Thames, Big Ben, and a 360-degree panorama of the city itself. It is quiet—much like the Corcovado—and a perfect place for me to reflect on what I have seen of Great Britain.

From its many cathedral spires to the Welsh cliffs and quaintness of the countryside, Britain is beautiful. Like the tea, however, its Christianity seems weak.

I think back to the words of Dylan Thomas—*Do not go gentle into that good night . . . rage, rage against the dying of the light.* It's wouldn't be quite fair to lump all British churches together. There are many that are active, that struggle to keep the doors open to their entire community—many that are trying to "rage against the dying of the light." They remain pinpricks of light.

I think of Patrick McDonald and Viva, of Alpha and the fledgling classes sprinkled across Wales and England. Perhaps a better analogy would be the ocean's tide—rushing in with the Welsh Revival of 1903 and slowly receding over the next sixty years. I think of Swansea Bay and its famous receding tide, which leaves mud, rocks, and seaweed exposed in its curious withdrawal.

Perhaps, like the tide, this decline is only temporary—maybe another revival is on its way. Perhaps, in a world of theories and theology, we are missing the obvious—maybe all Christ wants us to do is "feed the birds."

For a country with Christendom in its very bones, it seems like a return to active faith would be as simple as returning to a long-forgotten childhood home. Or would it? After all, as C. S. Lewis predicted, Britain's decline did not come suddenly; it overtook the culture slowly, with a combination of frustration, doubt, distraction, and numbness.

Perhaps someday soon, the water will return to give life to the most traditionally Christian country on the planet.

But at least for now, it seems, the tide is out.

Tanzania

wazunga in africa

I depart London's Heathrow Airport the next day. But it isn't until I look out the window of the plane and see nothing but sand that I realize: *I am really going to be in Africa in a few hours' time.* My next stop is Tanzania, in the heart of east Africa.

Home to approximately 40 million, Tanzania is one of the poorest countries in the world—in the bottom 10 percent of per capita income. Though it doesn't suffer the same degree of mass starvation as other African countries (like its neighbor Ethiopia), HIV and malaria are still significant matters of concern. One of the most diverse nations on the planet in terms of resources and wildlife, Tanzania is home to Mount Kilimanjaro, Serengeti National Park, and Ngorongoro Crater, among other natural wonders.

My hosts, Drs. Danny and Nancy Smelser, pick me up at the Kilimanjaro airport, which is un-airconditioned and dark. Danny is an emergency room physician and Nancy a nurse. The Smelsers are from the U.S. and have nearly finished their first year in northern Tanzania, where they have built a house and medical clinic called the Tanzanian Christian Clinic (TCC).

During the two-and-a-half hour drive to their home in Monduli, the Smelsers tell me about their mission. Their clinic is closed for construction at the moment but scheduled to open in six to eight weeks. Until then, they have stayed busy doing clinics out of the TCC mobile medical trailer.

When we finally arrive at their long, pothole-riddled driveway, it's apparent that rainy season has taken its toll: the Jeep bounces so furiously, Nancy and I both have to hang on to keep from hitting our heads on the ceiling. As I clutch the back of the seat and she grips the dashboard, a crate of soon-to-be-recycled Coke bottles behind me clink furiously, as if a party of ten were toasting our arrival.

Nancy kindly warns me to watch my step. "Please don't go anywhere at night without a flashlight," she adds, as Monduli is home to several deadly snakes. The Smelsers have been fortunate enough to avoid the deadly black mamba, but found a cobra on their clinic porch and another in the radiology room last month.

Specifically designed for houseguests working at the clinic, the Smelser home is a one-level, five-bedroom dwelling with a den, kitchen, and dining area. Nancy leads me to my room: a bare, yellow bedroom with a bed, a rug, and a rotating fan. The windows slide open to allow the night breeze to circulate between the metal bars; strange African noises also waft in—the muffled yips of jackals, monkeys, and hyenas.

Nancy cuts into my thoughts, warning me not to be afraid of voices in the yard. Because of all the construction on the clinic, a man named Samson and his team of watchmen guard the house and clinic at night with a large Maasai walking stick in hand. One night when the clinic foundation was being laid, Samson spotted a man who was stealing cinder blocks from the construction site and beat him with the stick. (If you saw Samson, you would know why this was effective.) He then rounded up some men to take the perpetrator to the police station, making him carry one of the cinder blocks as "evidence." Now, half a dozen local men guard the house in shifts each night.

Morning provides a clearer view of the Smelser compound. The house and clinic, trimmed in bright-orange gutters, stand alone in the middle of a shrub-filled prairie.

Monduli lies at the base of Mount Meru, surrounded by plains and the small volcanic hills marking the north border overlooking Kenya. The town has only a few main roads—most unpaved and of a dark, earthy brown—and one lonely gas station.

On my first afternoon, the Smelsers and I drive into Arusha, about a forty-five-minute drive from Monduli. Arusha is the third-largest city in Tanzania, behind the capital of Dar-es-Salaam and the city of Dodoma in the south. This area is home to 400,000 locals and considered the hub of the northern Tanzanian safari circuit—within driving range of several wildlife parks.

Everyone but us is a pedestrian. Danny and Nancy explain that they had quite a time getting a Jeep to drive. Since there is little credit in Tanzania, vehicles must be paid for in cash, then ordered from a dealer because there isn't enough demand for car lots. Vehicles on a lot would be too easy to steal.

As we turn onto the paved road leading to Arusha, we pass old men with walking sticks and groups of children dressed in school uniforms, playing in the ditch. Unafraid of the Jeep, they stop and stare at us as we pass. In general, the *wazungu*, or "white man," is a curiosity, but is respected wherever he goes. We proceed to a grocery store, which is guarded with rifles. This small store carries mostly essential dry goods in six short aisles. The candy bars—all Cadbury products—are under glass at the checkout as if they are prized gems.

Twenty years ago, there were no Western amenities like toothpaste and toilet paper in Arusha, Nancy says, although these can generally be purchased in Tanzanian towns of substantial size today. The average local salary is $50 to $80 a month, or about $2 a day.

Turning back on the road to Monduli, we pass several groups of straggling children. Children, or *watoto,* are allowed to wander freely here—a major concern to Danny when driving, as the Jeep tends to slip and slide on muddy roads.

When we arrive back at the house, Jill, the Smelsers' all-purpose housekeeper, is there with Samson and his wife, Charity, and the crew of clinic workmen. Meeting the Smelsers' staff is my first introduction to the curiosity of Tanzanian names like Mary, God Give, Prospero, and Witness.

Samson, his elongated earlobes displaying a hole about the size of a quarter, appears in the doorway to ask Danny a question. Samson is a native of one of Africa's most famous and highly revered tribes, the Maasai. Found mainly in southwest Kenya and northeast Tanzania, their trademarks are the cloak of red or purple cloth worn diagonally across the chest and the walking stick they carry with them at all times. Famous for hunting lions with spears, they are universally feared, and have been featured in

American movies such as *The Ghost and the Darkness* and *The Air Up There*.

The Maasai believe that the gods have entrusted all cattle into their care and have little respect for property boundaries. When they do settle down, they live in huts of dried cow dung and mud, arranged in circular villages called *bomas*. A warrior society, the Maasai are taller than most of their African counterparts, with genes that make them practically immune to heart disease and give them near-Olympic athletic prowess. "Modern Maasai" like Samson have adopted the street clothes and tin dwellings of mainstream culture.

After a few days with the Smelsers, I find I am learning several things about Tanzania very quickly. First, the most simple luxuries take a lot of work—clean clothes, hot water for showers—even brushing one's teeth requires using a glass of sterilized water. Whether the toilet will flush or the Internet will work is anyone's guess. Clothes cannot be left on the line overnight, as parasites will get into them. Dishes and vegetables must be rinsed in bleach water to kill bacteria.

Midweek, we rise bright and early for a mobile TCC clinic. The TCC is funded partly by the Smelsers and partly by their sponsoring congregation, Cross Point Church in Alabama, along with donations from various American organizations. The clinic staff includes two other American nurses, a local administrator, a translator, and a security officer. The motto of the TCC is "The healing of the whole man." Bible studies are arranged as a follow-up to patients who request prayer.

I ask Danny about some of the most common illnesses seen at the clinic. Milder ones include stomach worms, fungal infections (especially on feet), malnourishment, and eye infections. The more serious diseases include malaria, typhoid, tuberculosis, STDs, and HIV. The Smelsers initially struggled to determine what to charge for treatment. They didn't want to turn anyone away for lack of payment but were advised to charge a small fee and to insist that everyone pays, without freebies. Their flat fee for basic services is around $5 to $10 U.S.

Over time, the clinic has seen patients with ailments ranging from hypertension, asthma, pneumonia, and arthritis, to impetigo, shingles, schistosomiasis, pelvic disease, and liver failure. One five-year-old patient with severe malnutrition was the size of a toddler. One skeleton-like twenty-one-year-old man had a respiratory infection, a grossly enlarged spleen, and symptoms of TB, HIV, or cancer—if not all three. He had walked several miles, on no food, to arrive at the clinic at 6:00 a.m. to ensure being seen. Still awaiting an X-ray machine at the time, the Smelsers had no choice but to treat him with antibiotics, give him donated peanut butter to eat, a supply of clean water, and refer him to the nearest government hospital.

Nancy says many patients arrive at the clinic with blood pressure and/or sugar levels so high that they would be sent to intensive care in the U.S. Some are HIV positive. Many females arrive after being beaten by their husbands, with no legal alternative but to return home. Cases involving preventable maladies, especially in children, infuriate Danny, such as the nine-year-old girl who stepped on a fish skeleton at a local market and wound up having her leg amputated because the infection was never treated.

When the Smelsers are doing a mobile clinic, like today, they contact local churches in advance and ask them to announce it. The Smelsers' ten-person team includes myself, the local preacher, Justus, and a few others.

We pull up to a half-deserted school building surrounded by twenty yards of mud. The schoolroom floor is paved but dirty. As I sweep out the dust, I hear rats scuttling along the wall in the other room. Seven desks are stationed outside for assessing symptoms and taking vital signs. Patients then proceed inside to one of two makeshift examination areas and stop by the "pharmacy" on their way out. We are up to twenty-five walk-ins almost immediately—half of what we can see in a day. Soon we have a steady stream of people and all fifty time slots are handed out.

Multitudes seek the TCC's services. One young woman with Bell's Palsy (facial drooping) nearly cried when she finally received medicine that would ease her pain. One patient entered the clinic very ill from eating a cow she had found dead. Three other Maasai patients had each been attacked by wild animals. Malnutrition among infants is common. A newborn twin girl had been given to a woman who had never been pregnant and the infant was starving—her adoptive mother could produce no milk and was at her wits' end. One Maasai woman, six and a half months pregnant, traveled with her husband for three days from their remote village to reach the clinic, camping at various *bomas* along the way. She had delivered seven babies previously, but four had died.

Though we are only treating people's physical illnesses, the psychological effects of their suffering astound me. Most complaints at today's mobile clinic are minor, and the most common remedy is ibuprofen, though eyedrops and rash creams are also standard. We are out of FiberSure for bowel complaints in an hour. Most children seem to suffer from respiratory complaints or stomach worms.

A U.S. church has donated handmade teddy bears for the children, and I hand them out. I give one to a four-year-old orphan with stomach worms who was brought in by a concerned grandmother. The little boy stares at the teddy blankly. I realize he doesn't know what it is. He is unaccustomed to having toys.

The fiftieth patient is seen, and others, sadly, have to be turned away. Weary and exhausted, the team packs up the supplies for the drive home.

I shower that night with flip-flops on and my mouth closed, using bottled water to brush my teeth. I take my anti-malaria medicine, then cover my legs and ankles with bug spray before climbing into bed.

Today's clinic has put the American healthcare crisis in a new light for me. It's not perfect, but at least we *have* healthcare and ready access to lifesaving technology. In Tanzania, people have to wait for someone to come and hand them Tylenol for headaches.

In her best-selling book *Kisses from Katie*, American teen and Ugandan missionary Katie Davis once compared the need in countries like Tanzania to trying to empty the ocean with an eyedropper.

As sleep closes in, I have to admit, the bad news is, I believe this is true.

The good news is God has given every one of us an eyedropper.

paternalism vs. indigenous

as a country, Tanzania is roughly one-third Muslim, one-third
Christian, and one-third indigenous religions or no religion.
On Sunday, Danny, Nancy, and I drive to a church in Arusha.
Inside the one-room, pink concrete building with an outhouse
are a dozen rows of wooden benches. *Kanisa la Kristi* (Church of
Christ) and *Hukutana Hapa* (You Are Welcome) are written in
red, white, and blue letters above the entrance.

Contrary to popular belief, modern African fashion does not
mean "scantily clothed." The women are dressed in colorful,
mismatched garments—loose, baggy shirts with sleeves to the
elbow, long skirts, bright kerchiefs tied around their heads.
Danny jokes that the quickest way to cause a stir in Africa is to
wear a miniskirt, as it is considered improper to show one's legs.
There is no trace of cleavage—even the tops of women's arms
are covered. The men are dressed in dull-colored shirts and
khakis.

The people in the congregation take their seats, women on the
left and men on the right, with about forty in attendance. This

week's lesson is on Proverbs 1:7, "The fear of the Lord is the beginning of knowledge" (NIV).

About ten minutes into the sermon, I feel something at my side and discover an adorable little girl with short-cropped, tightly braided cornrows seated next to me, her large eyes studying me intensely.

I smile, and this is all the encouragement she needs. Her tiny fingers reach up to touch my earrings, then my hair. She proudly shows me a 25-shilling coin her parents gave her for the offering. She then searches my hands. When I hold them out to indicate I don't have an offering, she assumes I must have dropped it and starts searching the floor eagerly. It doesn't occur to her that I would come empty-handed. After all, if *she* has an offering, surely the rich foreigner must have one.

Determined to help me, my new friend starts lifting the skirts of women sitting next to us to look for my coin. Since I don't know Swahili, I don't know how to tell her to stop. She then enlists the help of other children, babbling animatedly in Swahili to search for the white girl's lost coin.

Eventually she does stop, disappointed that she couldn't find my offering for me.

As soon as the closing prayer is over, my little neighbor leaps up and bounds out the door to play with the other children. The Smelsers' Jeep is the only vehicle there. Besides two other American missionaries, Paul and Allie Carroll, the rest of the congregation has traveled on foot to get here.

The Carrolls have been in Arusha for two years, working with the local Church of Christ school of preaching. At lunch, I ask the Carrolls what has been hardest about humanitarian work in Africa. Rather than commenting about primitive conditions or limited resources, as I expect, Paul explains the two schools of thought regarding Third World countries—one dubbed *paternalism* and the other *indigenous*.

Paternalists believe in using foreign resources to aid native outreaches. "We have the resources to build a school or clinic," a paternalist would argue; "why not use them?" The indigenous, or "hands-off," philosophy believes what the locals have is what should be used for humanitarian efforts. So if the locals live in wooden houses with dirt floors, that's what their church should be made of, not concrete and air-conditioning. The same goes for how the missionaries themselves live. Everyone who attempts to do work in underdeveloped countries pretty much has to pick one of the two options, Paul explains.

Since the Smelsers are running a medical clinic, they tend to favor the paternalistic option. "If I am going to establish a functioning clinic, I need running water and electricity," Danny says. "I need the Internet for medical research." However, a clinic with Western technology requires a higher level of expertise to run than the locals are trained for. An advocate of the indigenous theory might argue that using local resources would ensure that Tanzanians could continue to operate the clinic on their own when the Smelsers return to the U.S. (The Smelsers are aware of this and hope to train others to continue the clinic work.)

The main benefit of paternalism is that you are able to accomplish more, faster, Paul says; growth is slower with the indigenous approach. However, with no money to compromise the outreach, indigenous missions can usually be continued without the missionaries. Mixing any kind of money with missions in Third World areas carries heavy consequences, Paul says.

One commonly related dilemma is whether or not to employ congregation members in one's clinic or ministry. "If I am going to hire someone to work in my home, why not give the job to someone at the local church?" Danny says. The Carrolls, however, feel differently. At one point during the past year, Paul realized that of the fifty people present at an Arusha church service, nearly forty were on the payroll of American missionaries in some form or fashion. As a result, the Carrolls decided to stop employing Christians in their home.

"But the church could construe this as, 'Why are you employing complete strangers when brothers and sisters in your own congregation need good jobs?" Paul says, grimacing.

Because the indigenous method in its strictest form mixes nothing foreign with the outreach, "you know people's motives are real," Paul explains, "and you know it can be sustained when you leave."

But progress can be painfully slow, he warns.

"You have to communicate to your supporters back home that it will be the difference between growing mushrooms and oak trees."

Ideally, the best approach would combine the two philosophies, but this is not as easy as it sounds. As much as the Smelsers and Carrolls have tried to find a balance, new dilemmas constantly present themselves.

I am still thinking about all of this as I get ready for bed that night. Can you fault the Tanzanians for having mixed motives when it comes to Westerners and the church? For them, it is more about sheer survival rather than living in comfort.

As I kick off my sandals, I ask myself the question missionaries and aid workers have been asking for years: *paternalist or indigenist? Live entirely like the natives and work with only available local resources? What harm is caused by having Western amenities in my home? Would I be prepared to spend* years *accomplishing what could be accomplished in months using Western resources? At what long-term cost to local community, sustainability?*

Tonight, the only conclusion I can come up with is that each person or group must choose what they believe is right and try not to judge those who do it differently.

There is room for different strategies in the service of God.

"never play chicken with a *daladala*" and other african proverbs

africa is home to a rich variety of proverbs:

Rain does not fall on one roof alone.

Only a fool tests the water with both feet.

And, *it takes a village to raise a child* (made famous by Hilary Clinton).

Some sound strangely familiar:

A bad coconut renders good ones bad.

You do not teach the paths of the forest to an old gorilla.

Others are colorful and humorous:

Clothes put on while running come off while running.

The day a monkey is destined to die, all trees get slippery.

And (my favorite), *Only when you have crossed the river can you say the crocodile has a lump on his snout.*

The next day, Danny and I drive into town for errands. Along the way, we pass a handful of *daladalas*—brightly painted vans that serve as the local bus system. Reminiscent of Scooby Doo and the Mystery Machine van, they were named because they used to cost a *"Dollar! Dollar!"* to ride. While the fare on most is relatively cheap—as little as 15 to 20 cents one way—daladalas are usually in need of maintenance and overstuffed with people, making them prone to breakdowns.

Instead of names or numbers for the buses, they have identifying phrases painted on them such as "A Friend in Need Is a Friend in Debt" or "Don't Worry, Be Happy." Perhaps most eerie is the collision Nancy witnessed between two daladalas named "The Lord Is My Shepherd" and "I Shall Not Want."

Sometimes the truth is stranger than fiction.

As we enter Arusha, the typical sights and sounds greet us: a street clogged with cars, men carrying sacks of grain, a woman balancing two stacked pails on her head. The names of some of the local establishments are as colorful as the buses. There's The Christian Bar, the God Is Great Grocery, The Storm and The Honeypot (bars), Precious Inn for Precious Stay, and the Arusha Fancy Store (selling curtains and cloth).

The road we take home is wide enough for two lanes, but functions as a one-way. Vehicles rarely pass one another, but when they do, it is common courtesy for one of them to pull aside and let the other go by—a measure no doubt adopted when rainy season makes the roads a mess.

"How do you know who is supposed to pull over first?" I ask Danny as a daladala approaches us from the opposite direction.

"There's no rule, I suppose," he says, trying to gauge the other driver's intention. *Left? Right? Left? Right?* When it becomes clear that the other driver is *not* going to stop, we pull over just in time to watch him hurtle past.

Looking down at my legs, I notice they are spotted with bumps smaller than mosquito bites—chiggers, Danny says. He advises putting clear nail polish on them—it suffocates the bug and keeps you from scratching.

If I escape Africa with no malady worse than chigger bites, I will consider myself fortunate.

The next day, Danny and Nancy take me to the Maasai Cultural Museum. Sunlight seeps through the museum's thatched roof, giving the clay statues depicting Maasai life an eerie glow. A colorful tribe, the men have elongated earlobes, while the women can be distinguished by their shaved heads and beaded collars. Maasai women are married (or "promised") as young as five or six years old, staying with their families until they are of childbearing age. Until recently, the young men of the tribe were required to kill a lion—the nemesis of all cattle—or (in some areas) a member of an opposing tribe as part of their initiation into the warrior brotherhood.

The Maasai drink cattle blood as a health drink, as noted in one museum display. Both male and female circumcision are practiced—Maasai males are circumcised around the age of eight as a rite of passage. Female circumcision is prohibited by the Tanzanian government but is difficult to enforce. Polygamy is a common practice too—usually men in the tribe will have up to three wives.

Our guide explains the significance of the Maasai walking stick and the different styles of cloth, which represent the phases of Masaai life—whether one is a juvenile, a warrior, a parent, married, widowed, and so on. A woman's beaded ruff, for example, usually indicates she is of childbearing age. Studying some of the jewelry, I ask the significance of one of the elaborate beaded bangled bracelets behind the glass.

The guide just looks at me quizzically. "Maasai fashion," he says simply.

That afternoon Danny, Nancy, and I go to midweek services at Monduli Church of Christ. The church is a large, one-room building of unpainted concrete bricks. The building is locked, and Nancy checks her watch as the time for scheduled services passes. At fifteen minutes past the hour, Justus, the preacher, rides up on a motorcycle, apologizing for being late.

A few other congregation members trickle in until there are ten of us present. Justus leads us in songs. My mind wanders as he begins the lesson in Swahili, a discussion of 1 Corinthians 3, "Divisions in the Church." The sky is becoming dark. It is not until the scenery outside the church begins to be enveloped in a brown, hazy fog that I realize—*dust storm*!

With Nancy's permission, I jump up to bolt the windows just in time. The others continue with the lesson as if nothing is happening. To me, a dust storm seems like a biblical mandate to stop the service, as if the book of Exodus is bearing down upon us. But I then realize that things like this that would be a big distraction in the U.S. don't stop the show in Tanzania. I look at the congregation, still focused on Justus, as the storm swirls outside. To put it in Nancy's words, "Would we be committed enough to walk for hours, enduring heat in the dry season and slogging through mud in the rainy season, only to sit in a 90-degree room for services?"

The storm lasts half an hour. Outside, the Jeep is caked in dust, but other than that, there is no sign that anything unusual has happened.

Back at the house, however, I look down at my legs to discover that the dust has stuck to the nail polish covering the chigger bites, making them look like large, brown bruises. I scrub hard, but it won't come off. Add this to the fact that I have managed to drop something heavy on two of my toenails, causing them to turn black, and my legs look downright diseased.

Oh well. In a continent of dust where bodies are marked by heat, chiggers, and travel on long roads, I now fit in perfectly.

ngorongoro crater and noah's ark

The book of Isaiah seems to come to life in Africa—stars, lions, cobras, grasshoppers, goats, straw, chaff, wells, warriors, desert, pools of water, mountains, bracelets, cloaks, potters and clay. Especially as we plan to visit nearby Ngorongoro Crater, the "Eighth Wonder of the World" and one of the premier safari destinations in Tanzania.

Originally a gigantic volcano, the ten- to twelve-mile crater was formed when the volcano collapsed inward. The crater is home to more than 30,000 animals; most species live year-round *inside* it, making it a natural fishbowl for safari-goers, with the densest known population of lions among its parks and more than twenty-five endangered rhinos.

Hoping to arrive at Ngorongoro by 10:00 a.m., we sleepily pile into the Jeep to begin the three-hour trek to Ngorongoro. I consult a trusty safari book that oozes enthusiasm for our journey: "*As you embark on your safari, consider how lucky you are to be witnessing these rare species in their natural habitat. The element of excitement in a safari is ever present; part of it, perhaps, is the potential for danger, but part is also the notion that you are on a voyage of discovery.*"[16]

It is still early, and as we drive along the main road, which is nothing but yellowed grass and telephone poles, Danny suddenly points out three giraffes grazing lazily thirty feet away. My first up-close encounter with a safari animal! The creatures move seemingly in slow motion, lending them a regal appearance. While we stop to watch, another herd appears on the left side of the road and then meanders across.

This brings us to "*Safari Rule #1: Don't get too close to the animals, and don't try to help them cross a perceived obstacle. You have no idea what they're trying to do or where they want to go.*"

Danny recranks the engine and we resume our journey. As we ride along, being pitched toward the ceiling every so often, Danny comments on the difference in this road since 1992, when the Smelsers suffered not one but three flats on the way to the crater. It's important to allow enough time to tour, because most parks open at dawn and close promptly at 6:00 p.m.—whether you are out of the park or not. If trapped inside the gates, you are pretty much forced to sleep in your car until morning, when a park ranger returns.

As we get closer to the crater, we pass under flowering jacarandas trees, with their bursts of bright red and purple. Vultures sit high above, looking down upon the bartering safari-goers with their idling jeeps. I imagine them talking in British accents like in *The Jungle Book*:

"They drive like Americans. Do you think they'll get eaten in the crater?"

"I say, look at the legs on that one. Brown spots!"

We slowly ascend the mountain. Nancy and I use the out-houses next to a dusty gas station straight out of the 1950s. For Ngorongoro to be a natural wonder, the commercialism that would have engulfed the area in the U.S. (think Grand Canyon) hasn't caught on *at all*.

When I come out, I am surprised to see six zebras casually strolling through the station as if they had walked out of a local zoo and arrived to help us pump gas. Seeing them at such short range reminds me of how little I actually know about zebras. *How close is too close? Should I get in the car?* I uneasily back toward the vehicle, but the door is locked. The zebras pass so close to the Jeep, I could have reached out to touch them, but I am afraid to make any sudden movements. I can feel the eyes of the gas attendants on me, and I know they are laughing at the girl from America who is afraid of zebras.

Danny soon comes out of the crater offices with our paper-work, followed by seventeen-year-old Tobias, our mandatory guide, who is training to go into Tanzanian tourism. Crater expert now present, we take the dusty, bumpy road into the crater. "Bumpy" might be a bit of an understatement—both hands are required to hold on to the seat as we are tossed around like popcorn in a popper. I start to worry that the road will actually tear up our car and we will be stranded in a field of lions.

The roads inside the crater are poor, but at least they're flat. There are only three or four places down there where visitors are allowed to get out of their vehicles: a rocky, sandy field upon entering, two picnic/rest areas, and one lone outhouse deep in the park. As we arrive at the first stop, the liability of what we are about to do dawns on me: we are in the middle of a field of wild animals with nothing between us and the animals.

All of a sudden, my common sense—which must have been dormant on the drive into the caldera—kicks in. *Bad idea. Haven't these people seen* Jurassic Park? For some reason, I had always pictured a safari as men in pith helmets armed with rifles on the back of a double-decker vehicle, not three unarmed civilians in a white 4 x 4 Jeep.

I briefly wonder how much it would take for the side of the car to be crushed by a charging rhino.

As our guide, Tobias is supposed to ensure that everyone stays inside the vehicle, but I can't help wondering, *If all the occupants decided to get out of the car at the same time, what could he really do to stop them?* Only in Tanzania would the honor system and a walkie-talkie be sufficient. I can just see a car full of fraternity boys from the University of Alabama wanting to get out and pet the cape buffalo. I wonder if they have pepper spray in Tanzania, and whether I should mention this to Tobias.

"*Immersion in the African safari lands is a privilege,*" the guide admonishes. "*Caution is your most trusted safety measure. Keep your distance, keep quiet, and keep your hands to yourself, and you should be fine.*"

Exempt from tourist laws, three Masaai men calmly stroll alongside a spring, watering their cattle, with an eclectic mix of zebras and warthogs nearby. On the other side, three suspicious Cape buffalo, their horns curved upward like a mustache, linger fifty or so yards from the vehicle—one in particular seems annoyed at our presence. "*Safari Rule #2: Never try to get an animal to pose with you.*" I try to imagine asking him, "Will you pose with me?"

"Cape buffalo are perhaps the least glamorous, but most deadly of The Big Five, as they generally kill more humans per year than lions, cheetahs, elephants or rhinos. Do be on the lookout for lone old males. These old guys can turn on a dime and run like lightning."

Buffalo are often attacked by lions, the book says, but taking down one buffalo usually involves several lions, so the lions are more likely to go after easier prey. The lone bull keeps eyeing us suspiciously as Tobias talks about kori bustards, the largest bird that can still fly that is native to Africa—one of which is hopping in front of the car. Driving on, we pass some warthogs, curious animals resembling pigs with horse's heads, and wildebeest, which look like bearded brown goats with stick legs.

Next we come to a herd of zebra, one hundred or so grazing in a field. A herd of zebra is a psychedelic thing to behold. Put twenty or more together at a close distance and it makes for an optical experience straight out of the 1960s. A primary prey of lions, zebras appear as one large animal to the color-blind lion. Their foals are actually brown and white, enabling them to go undetected in tall grass.

Farther down, we meet an ostrich alone in a field. This guy is eager to let us observe him, striking more poses than a red-carpet celebrity. "I'm too sexy for this field . . . too sexy for this field." He stops, turns his back to us and then swivels his head around dramatically.

After another mile or so, we suddenly see three curious mounds in the grass—lions!

"There's nothing quite like the feeling of first setting eyes on one of the Big Five—lion, buffalo, elephant, leopard, lion and rhino— in the African bush. Being just a few feet away from these majestic

creatures is both terrifying and exhilarating, even for the most seasoned safari-goer."

A sleepy male, looking like a large rock, groggily lifts his head, his autumn mane blowing in the breeze. He glances at our Jeep disinterestedly before laying his head back on his paws.

While we watch the inactive lumps in front of us, Tobias tells us more. The word for *lion* in Swahili is *simba*. Like many households, the females do most of the work, even gathering food for the entire pride, which usually consists of six to eight females and one or two males. The males fight with other males and eat what the females catch. Lionesses generally wait until after dark, when temperatures are cooler and visibility is low, to hunt. They prefer medium-sized animals such as zebras, buffalo, and wildebeest. Lions have no natural predators other than the occasional encounter with crocodiles, Tobias informs us. Their greatest threats are other lions and human hunters like the Maasai.

We stop for lunch at the hippo pool—fifty or so are submerged in the glassy water with only their backsides and the pink around their eyes and ears showing. This is one of the few places tourists are allowed out of the car. Visibility is good in all directions, but I still scan the horizon for any sign of approaching beasts.

Dead safari-goers tell no tales.

The Jeep once again kicks up dust as we trundle toward the far side of the crater. Suddenly, Danny reaches down and smacks the floorboard of the car and then opens the door abruptly. "A tsetse fly," he says in disgust. "I think it almost bit me." Bluish-green, almost like a mini dragonfly, tsetse flies are known to carry sleeping sickness. I look down at my own legs instinctively, but thankfully I have only the chigger bites.

After driving for some time, we come across another pride of lions sleeping in the rain. A lioness licks her cub as a juvenile male looks on. He has a short, spiky mane and what looks for all the world like eyeliner. I try to take his picture, but he just rolls his eyes.

About two hundred yards beyond the lions, we pull up to a bare, two-seat outhouse, shaded by trees. Tobias informs us that this is the last rest stop before the long trek out of the crater. *An outhouse in the middle of lion territory?* The outhouse is surrounded by tall grass. How do we know there aren't lions there, waiting to pounce on unsuspecting humans?

The call of nature eventually wins out, and I decide to make a run for it.

Literally.

Once we are back on the road to Arusha, I am able to reflect on the splendor of the crater. There is something both childlike and magnificent about watching animals. When we are young, we take in the world around us, but when we get older, our focus shifts to the human world and all its troubles. We plow through our day, barely noticing the wildlife around us—birds and squirrels in trees, bugs in the grass—but as the Lord sternly reminded Job, nature evidences God's majesty.

When the Apostle Paul writes about the gifts in the body of Christ, he uses the analogy of the human body, but after spending a day watching the circle of life in Tanzania, I think how easily he could have used the animal kingdom instead. For example, lions are the most glamorous, but they are among their own worst predators. They have limited vision and are unable to sprint for long. While it would seem that other animals are weaker, buffalo have their horns and the protection of their herd. Zebras have sharp eyesight and stripes for camouflage. Giraffes have powerful legs—one kick can crush a predator's skull. And this hardly scratches the surface of the capabilities and intricacies of each creature. Still, because of the way the food chain is intertwined, if one species suffers, the entire savannah suffers with it.

When playing zoo, most children want to be a lion—no one seeks to be a hyena or an anteater. And yet, how often do we foolishly throw away our own unique gifts trying to be the lion, someone we're not. Call it the "circle of life in the Spirit," if you will. "Serve each other according to the gift each person has received, as good managers of God's diverse gifts."[17]

Back at the house that night, Justus presents me with curious-looking red coffee beans. I turn the homegrown beans, which look more like berries, in my hand, thinking of Kaldi, the legendary discoverer of coffee, and his Ethiopian goat. Everything in Tanzania, it seems, is homegrown—from the coffee to the churches.

After being in the crater today, I have to say, the noises outside my bedroom window don't seem so scary. As the wild shrieks of animals combine with occasional shouts from the night watchmen, I eventually fall asleep, no longer concerned with whether the sounds are animal or human.

monduli-ju

The next day, we decide to visit Monduli-Ju, or "Upper Monduli," home of the primitive local Maasai. During a previous visit to a rural Maasai village, the elders asked Danny how to improve the health of their village. Danny advised them to do three things: wear shoes, dig latrines away from the water supply, and boil their water before drinking it. He also told them what the Bible admonishes about not drinking blood.

The elders discussed his advice, and one of them came back to Danny with this: "When we are sick and go to the hospitals, one of the first things you do is give us blood. We run the risk of getting HIV off your blood, so we think it is best to drink the blood of our own cattle and take our chances with getting diseases."

Well, you can't say this wasn't a thoughtful reply! And unfortunately, it is often true, as blood screening in Tanzanian hospitals is less stringent than in the U.S.

Today's visit is to the same rural area but a different Maasai boma. Samson, his wife, Charity, and Justus volunteer to accompany Danny and me to translate. Coming into the clearing,

eight huts are arranged in a semicircle around a cattle pen
made of twisting branches. The huts are made of mud and
cow dung, with the door frames made of branches. The conical
roofs are thatched with straw. After a few minutes, we
are greeted by three Maasai women. I try not to stare at their
graceful bald heads adorned with large, drooping earrings
bigger than their own ears. One wears a deep-blue dress with
a purple cloak, and another a brown wrap with one shoulder
bare, kind of like a seductive monk. They are all the wives of
one man—the village magician—who is not home, Charity
explains.

I look around warily for their spears. Charity tells them
Danny is a doctor and I am a visitor from the U.S. and she asks
if we can see inside one of the huts. *See* might not be the appropriate word. The tall wife gracefully beckons us to a nearby
hut, but as soon as we stoop to enter, we are immersed in pitch
darkness.

The huts are not one large room, but like the inside of a conch
shell, with mud walls curving and blocking the light from the
door. One of the wives produces a stool for me to sit on while
my eyes adjust to the dark. The smell of deep smoke chokes the
senses. With Danny, Charity, the wife, and one of the children
crammed inside, our gathering soon has the feeling of four adults
sitting inside a closet.

I am bursting with questions for the wives—*How many people
live in this hut? How old are you? How old were you when you
married?* Charity patiently translates the answers. Each wife has a
separate hut for herself and her children. The men bunk together,
or sometimes the husband alternates spending the night with each

of the wives. The women take turns cooking and watching the children.

This wife says she was about six when she was contractually married; she remained with her family until she was old enough to go live with her husband. I then ask about the marriage ritual. She tells me her parents took her to the market one day, and she went home with her husband. That was it. The other wives were married at eight and nine years old respectively. Between the three of them they've had eleven children, eight of whom survive.

Most Maasai do not know their exact age or birthday, so it is hard to ask about age or life expectancy—they just nod their head and say, "Many years." I ask what customs the Maasai have when someone dies. Some of it is lost in translation, but the part I am able to decipher is that they take the bodies far away from the bomas and leave them as food for the hyenas. The woman is very keen on emphasizing "far away."

By now, my eyes have adjusted enough to recognize a small pile of wood and a pot—apparently the cooking corner. The women cook *inside* the huts, with no ventilation. One reason eye disease is common among the Masaai.

I ask the women what the people of their boma believe about God, but all I can get is, "Yes, God." The idea of the Christian God competes with indigenous perceptions of God—the Maasai are willing to believe that a God of nature exists, but their specific theology stops there.

When we emerge from the hut, several men are awaiting our arrival—tall Maasai men who eye us, especially me, suspiciously. The tallest man is the husband of the three wives. Exactly what his position as "tribe magician" entails, we can't get out of him. He seems to be something between a witch doctor and pharmacist.

We settle on a patch of grass beside one of the huts, the wives tending three small children. We set up a three-way translation system so everyone can understand the conversation—Danny speaks in English, Justus translates to Swahili, and his friend Maki translates the Swahili into primitive Maasai. In other words, a game of "telephone." First, Danny asks some basic questions about their perceptions of God:

Where does God live?

No one knows this.

Who is God?

Your friend.

Who is the enemy of God?

Those who do not do his will.

We talk more specifically about God. One of the Masaai wives wants to know who the two men hanging on the cross with Jesus were—were they two of his friends? Danny briefly tells the story of the two thieves.

They are interested in talking more about God and, as a starting point, Danny begins . . . at the beginning, telling the creation story. As I listen I realize that in talking about my faith, I've never had to start at creation—those I've spoken to in the U.S. at least know about God, Jesus, and the devil—even if they didn't believe in any of them.

A small trickle of brown liquid winds its way on the ground toward our hands—one of the toddlers, who is wearing a long nightshirt and no diaper, has urinated in the grass. This marks another first for me—I've never had anyone pee on the ground during a Bible study.

When it's my turn to weigh in, in the circle, I wonder what's most appropriate. Will they think I'm crazy if I speak of the man who spent three days in the belly of a whale? The day the sun didn't go down? The burning bush? I try to think of which one they could relate to most, and what comes to mind is Daniel and the lion's den. I hit the high points of the story, telling specifically of how God sent angels to shut the lions' mouth so that Daniel survived all night—something I thought the Maasai might find impressive.

"The Maasai are used to killing lions by themselves with only a spear," Danny whispers to me. "That may or may not sound novel to them."

"Tell them Daniel didn't have a weapon of any kind," he instructs the translator. The Maasai faces display polite, unemotional interest.

"You will come back next week at 3:00 to teach," one of the wives declares upon finding out that Justus is a preacher. I don't ask how they will know the 3:00 hour exactly, but Danny agrees to return.

Afterward, we walk back to the Jeep where, upon finding out we are headed to the market, the wives politely ask for a ride. I confess, there has been no stranger feeling on this trip so far than sitting in a Jeep beside a well-oiled Maasai.

The market is a blur of men and women dressed in Maasai cloaks. There is a large pot brewing *pombe*, or banana beer, outside a crude, mud-caked shack, and large slabs of meat hanging by rope. Goat meat roasts on spears over a nearby campfire, while other stands sell baskets of eggs and fried bread. I wander among the crowd while Danny inspects some homemade rope for purchase. A grizzled old man tugs at his beard as he watches me.

We are quiet on the way home, tired and thoughtful. I ask the Smelsers what they believe it would take to bring Tanzania out of poverty. It would require eliminating government corruption, they say, and improving basic infrastructure such as schools and paved roads, and capitalizing on tourism. If you did this properly, you could probably run the entire country off tourism, Danny says.

Central and southern Africa are generally considered the poorest continental regions in the world, with approximately 50 percent of the world's poor living there. Many Westerners believe that offering enough money and resources would "fix" Africa once and for all. However, I am now realizing, as those who work in Africa will tell you, the solution is much more complex.

In the recent book *Dead Aid*, author Dambisa Moyo, a Harvard graduate and native African, asks the questions the rest of the world is wondering: Why, after *decades* of aid, is the problem not any better?

Experts generally agree on four root causes. The first is government corruption. Public funds and international aid money are frequently pocketed or used for the military while the rest of the country suffers poor roads, few sewage or irrigation systems, and insufficient water supply. In many cases the cor-

ruption exists right down to the city licensing board or electric
company, leaving citizens to pay bribes for standard services.
Second, there is confusion over land rights—what is public
versus private property? The absence of an infrastructure leaves
the population defenseless against the harsh climate and natural
disasters such as famine and drought. Third, political instability
also leads to frequent civil war, making it difficult for development and creating refugee problems. Finally, disease is devastat-
ing—from HIV/AIDS to insect-borne illnesses to diseases from
unclean water.

Everyone agrees that the corruption needs to be eliminated
first. Then, the other priorities include: relieve extreme hunger,
establish a clean water supply, decrease disease, provide access to
education, and improve public services.

While celebrities and nonprofits continue to raise money for
these causes, a new movement is questioning whether Western
aid in general is helping or hindering growth. We've been told
that raising money is the noble thing to do. But what if just giving
money is the *lazy* thing to do?

Moyo uses the example of providing free mosquito nets, which
aid in preventing malaria, to illustrate this point: Suppose a local
mosquito-net manufacturer employs ten people, producing five
hundred nets per week—more than enough to keep his town
and the surrounding countryside supplied. Then, some well-
intended celebrity raises support to send 100,000 mosquito nets to
the region from the West. The local manufacturer can't compete,
and his factory is shut down. However, in five years, most of
the donated mosquito nets will no longer be usable, and yet the
region will need functioning nets, meaning that aid will have to

again come from somewhere. Meanwhile, a local factory could have evolved to fill the need permanently.

Almost everyone agrees that change is needed. Giving and raising money are not easy, but they are the *easiest* of all the solutions at our immediate disposal, so that's what we continue to do. But what if simply throwing money at the problem is *never* going to fix it?

I ask myself, *Do we have a moral obligation to help poor countries?* Yes. *But it is ethical to help in a way that multiplies the problem?*

I believe we owe it to the poorest regions of our world to be informed about the problems, not just write checks. Look for projects that provide education or stimulate the local economy. Give money directly to individual missionaries who are responsible and ethical with their resources, like the Smelsers, so that monies don't get diverted by government bureaucracy.

One of the biggest myths the Western church often perpetuates is that if you put money in the offering plate, you're off the hook. You need to do nothing more to improve the world around you. When this happens with governments taking a similar approach, dumping money in existing channels rather than digging new ones, we can see the hazards of that behavior.

There are many complicated answers to America's role in developing countries, but in the words of one African proverb: "The tree will be known by its fruit."

As I bid good-bye to Africa, I think about the Smelsers calmly sharing their faith with the Maasai, and about the TCC—just one drop in the vast bucket of Africa—bringing medicine to the multitudes, and I recognize the beautiful fruit of that tree.

China

the middle country

At the Kilimanjaro Airport the next morning, the power goes off four times, making what should be a simple luggage check-in process take an hour. As I depart Tanzania, there is a cry of "Kili" from the right side of the plane—a sighting of Mount Kilimanjaro, beloved by the locals. It is a surreal sight—a carpet of white clouds so thick you could almost stand on them, and the mountain's blue-and-white tip peeking through as if it were only a tiny hill.

My next flight is a 747 bound for Delhi, then continuing to China. I could not write about exploring Christianity around the world without mentioning the blossoming of Christianity in China, where I am visiting two friends in separate provinces.* Nicknamed "The Middle Country," China is the world's most populous nation, with more than 1.3 billion people. It is also the world's most atheistic country, controlled by the iron grip of its Communist government.

---

* Due to the sensitivity surrounding certain aspects of Christianity in China, all people and locations will be anonymous.

China's most famous landmark, The Great Wall, snakes for an impressive four thousand miles along the country's northern border. Symbolic in so many ways of China's attempts at isolationism, it remains the longest man-made structure ever built, constructed of brick, mud, stone, and wood. The wall is thirty-five feet tall at its highest remaining point, reduced to vandalized rubble and graffiti in other areas. It winds closest to the cities of Datong and Beijing.

As China's capital and second-largest city, Beijing is the seat of the Communist government—home of "The Forbidden City" and neighboring Tiananmen Square. Built more than six hundred years ago, The Forbidden City is the world's largest remaining palace complex, with more than nine hundred buildings. It was here that China's last emperor, the six-year-old child emperor Pu Yi, lived until his abdication in 1912. Regional warlords fought for control of the government until Mao Zedong founded the People's Republic of China in 1949.

Mao Zedong is known for both uniting and ruining China—depending on who you ask. He instituted "land reform" to revive the failing economy by confiscating farmland from the wealthy and redistributing it among peasants, a process that some estimate killed more than a million landowners. Others who were perceived as a threat to the new regime were also killed, snuffing out another million lives by conservative estimates.

Mao instituted China's first "Five-Year Plan," using Soviet aid to build new manufacturing plants and bring all industry under government control. To speed things up, he then created the "Second Five-Year Plan," billed as the "Great Leap Forward," which reorganized society under shared ownership, creating labor commues to replace the role of the family, resulting in a massive backfire, with famine and mass starvation.

In continuing efforts to stamp out lingering opposition to Communist ideology, Mao launched the infamous Cultural Revolution in 1966. He eliminated the class system by closing all educational institutions and ordering intellectuals to the country-side to be "retaught" the lessons of manual labor. He also declared war on what he called the Four Olds: Old Customs, Old Culture, Old Habits, and Old Ideas. This involved closing religious insti-tutions, destroying books, art, and historical artifacts, even valued family photos. People were encouraged to turn in neighbors and friends—anyone found in noncompliance.

Nationwide chaos ensued, and the army had to be dispatched to restore internal order in 1967. By 1970, the country was recov-ering from the purge, and education was slowly being reinstated, but the revolution would not fully end until Mao's death in 1976.

Back on the plane, concerns about swine-flu ripple through the passenger bay. Due to a recent epidemic, I'd heard rumors about Chinese airports scanning passengers' body temperatures as they arrived from international flights. Sure enough, before we land, flight attendants hand out cards with questions ranging from "Please list any symptoms you have had in the past two weeks" to "Have you been with pig recently?" Upon landing, four Chinese airline personnel board the plane dressed in white, hooded hazard suits. They politely make their way through the rows, scanning all three hundred passengers on the forehead with an infrared gun. I don't know about anyone else, but this makes me feel like a can of green beans at the grocery store. Miraculously, no one on the plane has a fever, and the four officials disembark to relieved applause.

My friend Lisa meets me at the airport exit, where we hail a taxi. Adventurous and cosmopolitan, Lisa has lived in China for seven years and learned a decent amount of Mandarin. The urban scenery picks up as we approach the city, and I notice the array of vehicles going under an overpass—a blue bus, a yellow taxi, a man on foot pulling a huge cart laden with white sacks, a moped.

Lisa's apartment is white-walled and modern. Due to China's large population, there are very few houses in the cities, only apartments. Looking at the urban landscape is somewhat deceptive, however, as up until the past thirty years, nearly 80 percent of China's population were farmers. Today, this number has fallen significantly—yet nearly one in every two Chinese still live off the land. Since the land in western China is either uninhabitable or ill-suited for agriculture, most Chinese are forced to live on the eastern half of the country. *Forced* is not an understatement, as permission from the government is needed to move to another region.

On the way to dinner, I stare out the window of our taxi, wondering: *In a city of millions, where do they put all these people?* This question is answered as we pass skylines of nondescript, cloned condos. Soon we are whizzing through the streets at breakneck speed, the lights of the city whirring past like a ride at Disney World. While I am contemplating the seeming inevitability of death by taxi, every now and then I notice a moped weaving in and out of the melee. *You couldn't pay me to ride one of those*, I think, watching the happy lunatics dart between cars.

Two days later, I find myself gliding through the streets of one of the city's large corporate complexes on the back of a moped. Faced with the dilemma of giving a taxi directions in Mandarin (which I can neither speak nor write) or hitching a ride through the back streets of the city on a moped with one of Lisa's friends, I have chosen the moped.

To gain more perspective on Christianity in China, I am meeting with Roger, an expert on China's first government-sponsored Bible printing press. The status of the church in China has varied *greatly* from decade to decade, making tales from the early 1980s very different from those in more recent decades.

Before coming to China, I had read books such as *Safely Home* and *The Heavenly Man* (both banned in China), which made me envision all underground churches meeting in caves during the early morning. Church leaders risked their lives. Forbidden Bible texts were passed around in weathered scraps. However, I had heard more recent visitors to China talk of church retreats, youth group meetings, and Steven Curtis Chapman concerts. When a friend mentioned that she had purchased a Mandarin Bible as a souvenir there, I was thoroughly confused.

"The church in China has many faces, like most countries around the world," Roger says, hands folded. "The century of 1850 to 1950 is the old-fashioned missionary period in China."

Once Mao's Cultural Revolution was underway, all missionaries were swiftly deported, he says. Religious activity could result in beatings, imprisonment, and torture. Instead, citizens were encouraged to carry a copy of quotations by Mao, known as "The Little Red Book," for memorization. It was a very dark time for the Chinese church.

At the end of Mao's reign, churches were allowed to reconvene, provided they registered their assembly with the government. This is still required today, as unregistered churches or home meetings are still illegal. Bibles are no longer forbidden—you can generally buy them from any registered church—but availability is still a problem.

Because the greatest taboo is to criticize the government, registered churches are restricted from preaching judgment upon those who are not Christians. Chinese citizens may bring visitors to church, but no religion is permitted to openly mass-evangelize (hand out pamphlets, make door-to-door visits, etc.). Roger says millions of Christians meet in unregistered fellowships, although the term *underground* is debatable. "Ninety percent are probably known," he says. "The Public Security Bureau keeps them in check if they cross over the line."

"Why do they go through all the trouble to meet in secret if it isn't a secret?" I ask.

"Well, people were badly wounded as a result of the Cultural Revolution," he explains. "Some of those who went through it have not gotten over that loss of trust. Many who choose house churches today have a strong distaste for the government."

"Pride is also a factor," he says. "They take the Great Commission—and [the fact] that they can't openly evangelize—very seriously. They think government-registered churches are not Christian."

House-church persecution varies widely from region to region, he says. Group behavior that is overlooked in a coastal location may not be tolerated in a rural village.

Government-registered churches are called Three Self Patriotic Movement churches (TSPM, or "Three Self" for short). As indicated by the name, these congregations are required to be self-leading, self-supporting, and self-propagating. The government also mandates that member churches forgo any denominational branding, worshiping instead under the general branches of *Catholics* or *Protestants*.

On the way back to Lisa's apartment, taxis whiz through the streets like large bobsleds, oblivious to passing lanes, turn signals, construction codes, pedestrians, or moped riders. I stop to buy some Light Coke (*Diet Coke*)—a telltale sign of an American, I'm told—fingering the multicolored Chinese *remimbi* (RMB) as I pay. Mao Zedong's face is on every bill. Though he has been dead for more than thirty-five years, his image is still everywhere.

"The revolution tore the culture apart," Lisa says. "Mao did some basic things—he simplified the language and built roads. But he set himself up as God, so that when he died, it created a vacuum. I think that's why Christianity has spread so quickly."

As I shower and get ready for bed, I think about the millions of Chinese going about their business every day, deprived of God and longing for hope.

Can you have one without the other?

three self

I awake the next morning to the sounds of construction. This is typical, as most of the large cities in China are under perpetual construction. The car horns are melodic musical instruments—and I lay there for several minutes, listening.

Today Lisa and I are going to services at a local Three Self Church. This particular church started about ten years ago, primarily with a group of teenagers. A few years later, it gained children and adults, and they began meeting in houses. When attendance grew, they registered with the TSPM and began meeting in an official building.

The building has a parking lot of bicycles. Inside, the church is white and undecorated, but air-conditioned. There are about 250 in attendance, and the audience is mostly Chinese, with about one-third foreigners. As the service begins, the words to the first hymn appear on a screen. Two Chinese women lead the singing—"Come Thou Fount of Every Blessing," followed by "What a Wonderful Maker." Then another woman reads Isaiah 61, "The Year of the Lord's Favor."

The sermon is taken from Genesis 12, "Is anything impossible with God?" The speaker recounts the story of Abram's calling, including Abram's various pleas for help and mercy—"If you ask God respectfully, he will respond to you," he admonishes. "But if you complain, he will rebuke you." After the sermon, there are concluding announcements, including a video advertising a Focus on the Family program.

On our way out, I see that half the lobby is dedicated to childcare, and in the other half, teenagers are selling T-shirts, Bibles, Christian books, and CDs. This is the only place to buy such items, as there are no Christian bookstores.

I think back to my visit with Roger. Advocates of Three Self churches would argue that it's easier to advance Christianity in China by working with the government—to a point—rather than fighting it. If the church is allowed to propagate peaceably, they argue, more freedom may be granted in the future. However, Brother Yun, one of the most famous house-church leaders in China, offers a differing opinion: "We see the Three Self believers as caged birds. Yes, they are able to sing, but their environment is controlled and their wings are clipped."[18]

After church, I go to the market with Lisa in one of the downtown areas. The market is a mixture of cheap and traditional goods, with the occasional pagoda and colorful lanterns with red tassels. We walk down pollution-soiled sidewalks beneath power lines stuffed so full of wire that they look as if they might burst. Ornamental archways lead down dingy, crowded alleys peppered with plastic rain umbrellas—a humorous sight in the scorching sun. The Chinese carry them to shield themselves from the rays.

While our taxi crawls along in bumper-to-bumper traffic on our way home, one of my worst fears happens— our taxi hits a cyclist, who smacks the front bumper with a jolt. Lisa and I both gasp. Our driver gets out . . . to see if the *taxi* is OK, bellowing at the biker, who tries to wobble away amid the traffic as quickly as possible.

When traffic picks up, we are once again merging in and out of lanes at faster speeds than necessary, cars honking. I brace myself with one hand against the seat in front of me. As I stare at the cityscape, it is mostly gray, but red is the main color in China— and it is everywhere—followed by yellow, the traditional color of the emperor. It all gives the streets the look of a gray canvas sprinkled with the contents of a child's crayon box.

Thinking back on the Three Self visit, I ask Lisa the question on every American's mind: "In general, how do the Chinese view their lack of freedoms?"

"The short answer is, most Chinese don't know they're not *free*," says Lisa, pitching forward slightly as we come to a near stop.

I stare at her blankly. "How can you *not* know you're not free, with all the regulations and lack of individual rights?"

"Well, the Chinese don't question things. They're not taught different perspectives," Lisa says.

"How much freedom of choice do they have?"

Lisa outlines the typical scenario for modern Chinese. "When you're young, you go to school. Few people get to go to college.

There's a list of colleges you can attend based on your test scores. In general, you don't date until after college. The Chinese are discouraged from marrying until they are nearly thirty. And when they do date, it's with a purpose, less recreational," she says.

Marriages are still arranged in certain parts of the country, but in urban areas, dating is common, she says.

"You can't move wherever you want to," she continues. "Otherwise, everyone would want to live in the large cities. Housing is assigned based on your job. You can't really move from city to city without a work permit."

And when the time comes to start a family, couples are only allowed one child, at the risk of paying a fine the average citizen can't afford. There are a few exceptions, she says, such as if you live in the country where you need children to perform manual labor, if you are part of a minority group, if your first child is handicapped, or if your firstborn dies.

I get to hear more about the Chinese perspective that afternoon at a nearby Bible study from Katie, a Chinese national in her late twenties.

"Christianity is becoming huge in China," she says. "Since 2005, things have been changing a lot. Christianity is not considered Western anymore. It is finally coming out into the public.

"The Chinese government has started taking the Christian house church movement seriously. They don't know how to deal with it, but they are very serious about the number of people in a church."

Katie recounts an example of two large churches in Shanghai and Beijing—one with eight hundred people—that rented office buildings in which to worship. Believing that the churches were getting too large, the government forced the landlord to stop renting the property to them rather than cause a scene. "They try to deal with it in indirect ways," she explains. "They don't want an international incident."

Due to space constraints, most house churches are hard-pressed to include more than twelve to fifteen people at a time. Once meeting attendance approaches twenty, the church is usually forced to split off, raising up a new leader for the new "congregation."

"After 1989," Katie tells me, "lots of students became Christians and then house-church leaders. The government doesn't like this—they equate Christianity with a democratic movement. Now, many students become Christians in college and feel called to full-time ministry. However, most stay in the city and try to register with the government. They don't want to be underground."

She adds, "The teaching in the Three Self Church is not all bad. They have their strengths and weaknesses. Pastors are very restricted by the government, and they receive pastors from seminaries within their system. Some deny miracles, don't believe in the Virgin Birth, and have been known to compromise because of politics. As a whole, I don't believe in their theology, but I do believe some pastors are trying to bring people to Christ."

I must say, if Christianity in America is a mocha frappe, in China it is a bitter tea.

Of all the countries I've been to, the prosperity gospel simply doesn't seem to exist in China. China is the first country where the concept of "come to Christ and your life will get better" really doesn't seem to apply. Thus the breed of believers China produces—as in all other countries where Christianity is persecuted—is markedly different. There is an element of "earthly expectation" missing from their faith.

In *Safely Home*, a fictional book describing the house-church struggle in China, Chinese character Li Quan sums it up best when he tells American Ben Fielding, "If you are looking for a religion centered around yourself, Ben, I must agree that Christianity is a poor choice. . . . Where did he promise you would not suffer? I can quote many scriptures where he promised we would suffer. Is it God you have rejected? Or have you turned from a false god created in your own image?"[19]

It is a question I hear travel across the ocean and echo on the shores of North America.

house church

The Yangtze River basically splits China into north and south. Henan is China's most populous province, in central China, with 97 million people living within its boundaries. The heartland of China's civilization for millennia, three of the largest house-church networks began there.

Depending on how you measure the urban areas, the largest cities in China are Shanghai, followed by Beijing, Tianjin, Guangzhou, and Wuhan, respectively. Perhaps the best example of "modern China," Shanghai is not only China's largest city but the largest city proper in the world, with a population of more than 19 million (greater than New York City, London, and Los Angeles combined). Originally a fishing town, Shanghai quickly grew to be one of the world's busiest international seaports, famous for "The Bund" waterway and skyline.

The next day, I visit a Chinese house-church retreat, minus Lisa. Surprisingly, the atmosphere looks pretty much like what I remember of church retreats in college—there are thirty-five or so students stuffed into one modest-sized room. A nearby chalkboard outlines the schedule—a morning prayer, then guys and girls split for separate hour lessons, then an hour of worship followed by an afternoon scavenger hunt.

There are a few hand-drawn posters depicting "Before Life in Christ" and "After Life in Christ," and a wash line strung across the room, to which participants have clipped notes of encouragement with brightly colored clothespins. I sit in on the singing, as attendees request songs from a small, photocopied booklet—"Lily of the Valley," "Prepare Me to Be a Sanctuary," and "God Is Love." The guest speaker is a traveling Chinese preacher who reiterates the characteristics of "Life in Christ, Before and After."

After the lesson, I am introduced to Ian, who has been a believer for nine years. "My story is pretty common," he says. "I began studying the Bible, and after several months, I became a Christian. After I was baptized, my life changed. Through the years I began to understand what the traditional Christians want to protect.

"The story of the church in China began in 1949 when the Communist Party decided it would lead the church," he says. "Two groups emerged—one that said, 'We will accept this,' and one that said, 'We will not accept.' From that time on, it has been divided."

I ask Ian why he chose to attend a house church instead of the Three Self Church. "The only leader of the church is Jesus Christ," he says. "This is very fundamental, so we should not accept the Three Self Church."

While some house churches do register, Ian estimates that 90 percent are unregistered. "The government tolerates it on the condition that you worship quietly," he says. "A big group is forbidden. Otherwise, you will know the power of the government."

"Have you ever been threatened or warned by local officials?" I ask.

"I don't care about that as long as I know I am on the right side," Ian says matter-of-factly.

When I ask him his opinion of Americans—"Strong in their faith, or not so strong?"—Ian pauses with a contemplative sigh. "Maybe I prefer the second option," he says slowly. "I'm crazy about the old, old America. Men like Washington and Jefferson who were chosen to be president but gave up their power to return to their farm. They did not try to grasp power or authority."

He smiles. "Americans used to be very lovely in my idea."

After the retreat breaks, I join Lisa downtown for an authentic, full-hour Chinese massage (cost: 60 RMB, or roughly $15). The Chinese art of Tui Na, a deep, kneading, continual massage, goes back for centuries.

The receptionist takes us to a room with four massage tables. We change into the provided red-silk PJs with ruffles, and a few minutes later, four dainty Chinese women enter. I am wondering if they have brought us tea, but it turns out they are here to massage us. I hardly have time to look at my masseuse before I am flipped over, face pressed into the "O"-shaped cushion. Within thirty seconds she has found the trouble in my neck and proceeds to forcefully rub—no, *mash*—the muscle against the backbone to break it up. It then becomes clear to me that this five-foot, middle-aged woman has more strength in her elbow than most grown men.

She then presses her elbow into my sacrum, which brings tears to my eyes. I wanted to yell "Uncle," but no one would have known what it meant. She deftly seizes one of my arms and pulls it behind me, as if she were ripping the wings off a butterfly. She leans over me.

"OK?" she asks cheerfully.

"OK," I croak weakly.

She motions for me to roll over, and before I can look my assailant in the eye, she has picked up my head in her hands. When she starts to massage my scalp, my head wants to melt off my neck. There has never been anything as blissful as this—flowers, fields, and white rabbits dance across my closed eyes. Beside me, I can hear Lisa's sinuses draining.

Massage over, I lie on the table in a heap, too relaxed or beat up—I can't tell which—to move. When I hear Lisa stirring, I drag myself up off the table and begin changing back into my street clothes, stars still dancing in front of my eyes.

When the morning comes, I feel surprisingly not sore. I sit in Lisa's small kitchen, bathed in sunlight, drinking chai, thinking about how the Chinese can be so humble and accepting of everything. While atheistic, there is something almost spiritual about their contentment in the face of hardship. I also think back on Tanzania, where life is turbulent for different reasons, yet its citizens also seem to weather the hardships of life better than those in the West.

Is it expectations, then, that determine a person's contentment level? Maybe.

Expectations for life in the West are certainly higher. The more I think about it, however, it seems the word at the root of it all is "control." The greater control people think they have over their life, the greater the problem of pain—or feeling of injustice—when things don't work out.

When I was nine, my best friend, Ginger, and I decided to make scrapbooks of our future lives—what we would wear and drive, what house we would live in, right down to the appliances in our kitchens. We even included pictures of our future children. We gave ourselves a weekly budget and went to work picking out bedspreads, dishware, jewelry, and lawnmowers. We spent hours clipping the Sears catalog and gluing our dreams into tattered, neon-colored notebooks.

If this sounds a little bizarre, I should add that our parents actually encouraged this activity at the time: they thought it promoted fiscal responsibility, and it entertained us for hours. Still, I admit . . . it was absurd.

But how many of us keep invisible notebooks of our future lives in our head from the time we are children? There is an illusion of control—the expectation of the life we'll have, or feel we *should* have—and when life disappoints, we are left feeling bewildered. Hurt. Because like nine-year-old Mandy and Ginger, we were trying to control things we really can't. Yet the freedom in our society makes us *believe* we can control these things—unlike the Chinese, who can't move anywhere, can't have a career, can't have more than one child, can't even turn on the air conditioner in the summer without government permission.

After visiting the church in China, it's easy to see why thousands are flocking to unregistered house-church fellowships.

They want *control* over how they worship, even if it's illegal. It's a freedom many Americans take for granted—hopping from church to church based on worship style, Bible studies, driving distance, the size of the young-marrieds group, and so on.

Does having "control" over your life make you happier? Don't be so quick to say yes.

It's a question you might want to ask the Chinese.

chinglish

When my stay with Lisa is over, I travel to another province to visit Kyle, a friend who has been working in China for two years. I am the only "foreigner" on my flight, evoking stares both at the terminal and on the plane. This does not deter the young Chinese man sitting next to me from giving me his business card and trying to pick me up. He knows English, so we have a brief conversation. When I ask him what he thinks about Christianity, he laughs. "That's for the older people. I think the young people find it hard to believe."

Kyle meets me at the airport, where he rescues me from a line of drivers offering to help with my baggage. Thankfully, Kyle is semifluent in Mandarin and is able to give orders to the driver.

To say that the Chinese language is difficult would be an understatement; the language uses various tones to communicate different meanings of the same syllable. (And while the language predates Communism, there is something ironic about the fact that even the tone in which one must speak is predetermined.) For example, *Ma* in a steady or flat tone means *mother*. Spoken

in a low to high tone (Ma?), it means *hemp*. Uttered in a falling
to rising tone (Ma-ah?), it means *horse*, and in a high to low tone
(Ma . . .), it means *scold*. Because the tone is already decided, it
often sounds to untrained ears like the Chinese are angry, when
they are simply communicating a fact. Needless to say, proper
pronunciation is key. I find this out when attempting to tell our
taxi driver "Thank you" (*xie xie*), accidentally saying the word for
"little girl's pee" instead.

After being let out of the taxi, we walk to Kyle's apartment,
which would be considered "ghetto" in the U.S. "You only get
an elevator in your building if it has more than seven floors," he
explains as we huff and puff, dragging the suitcases up the outdoor stairwell to his sixth-floor apartment. Curious floating seeds
looking like feather down waft through the air from the tops of
the trees, as if it were raining chickens.

Kyle knocks on the door of some Western neighbors in the
building, Ben and Ellen. As with other countries, lunch is the primary meal in China. It is so important that "Have you eaten?" is
a standard greeting. The other party is expected to answer "Yes,"
or "No, but I plan to eat shortly."

"Have you eaten?" Kyle hollers through the door. Ben and
Ellen say no. But there is a Japanese/Thai restaurant nearby they
have been wanting to try.

My first lesson about being a pedestrian in China is that cars
do not slow down for you. *At all*. Hesitate for any reason, or trip
on your shoelace, and you're a bug on the windshield. My clothes
are damp with sweat by the time we get to the restaurant, which
involves dashing across several major intersections one lane at a
time, Frogger-style. At Kyle's suggestion, I order the pork noodle

soup. This was not a well-thought-out choice for a chopstick amateur like me. On the list of foods to eat with chopsticks, I have ordered something at the medium-to-expert level.

The pork is fairly easy to manage, but the noodles are not long enough to wrap around the chopsticks, falling back in the bowl instead with an embarrassing splash. I ask for a fork. Even after Kyle has translated this to the waitress, her blank stare remains. She looks at me as if I have asked for a sippy cup. There are no forks.

"No problem," I say with a smile. *How big a deal can it be to eat with chopsticks?*

A minute later, the chopsticks are on the floor. Kyle has to flag down the waitress again. *Can we have another set of chopsticks?* She casts me another pitying look. Clearly, this American is incapable of feeding herself. By the time I have figured out a suitable eating method, which basically involves impaling the noodles and pork on one chopstick and eating it like a kebab, everyone else is finished.

One of the most frustrating cultural differences to outsiders is the Chinese custom of "saving face." As with many cultures where material possessions are scarce and all one has is one's good name, the worst thing you can do socially is to insult a person's honor. What is not obvious, however, is the degree to which the Chinese take it: they will seek to avoid anything that deviates from an ideal encounter. For example, when asked for something they cannot deliver, the Chinese businessperson replies, "I'll look into it and get back with you," rather than a straightforward, "I can't do that."

We witness saving face in action when Kyle stops by his employer's to reserve a meeting room. The management keeps trying to persuade him to meet at a different venue, which won't work at all for Kyle's purposes. He later finds out that the reserved room has a hole in the floor. The management can't get it fixed in time, so instead of just telling him that, they try instead to get Kyle to have the meeting outside.

Back at the apartment, Kyle tosses his keys onto a table and wearily plops down on the couch. Another of his friends, Holly, has joined us and the mood lightens when she produces a menu from a Western restaurant to cheer him up.

For some reason "Chinglish," as the translation from Chinese to English is jokingly called, tends to lend itself to especially bad grammar. Some of this can be blamed on poor translation, but part of it is a difference in the way the Chinese and Americans speak.

Some examples that Kyle and Holly have found:

> *The ancient building is renovating. Please excuse me for bringing trouble to you.*

> *The act of smoking, eating, and drinking the drink and staying on for a long time become troubled of other users and stop it, please.* (sign on subway)

> *Sale—100% off.*

> *Keep your legs no running.*

> *Attention. Don't jumping in elevator. If you do it, it's gonna be stop. And you must be locked up.*

Do not put the plastic back in your head to prevent from suffocating.

Please remove your shoes before being entered. Thank you.

"Chinglish" may be humorous, but the differences in the way Eastern and Western culture think are crucial for Westerners to understand. The main difference can be summed up as *individualism* versus *collectivism*, or communal society. For example, in China everyone celebrates their birthday on Chinese New Year, turning one year older "together." This well reflects the priorities of Chinese culture.

Where Americans tend to value self-expression, entrepreneurship, imagination, and emotion, the Chinese value loyalty, obedience, self-discipline, thrift, humility, and moderation. What Americans may think is a "weaker" set of values is simply what the Chinese have needed to survive for decades, for until the 1950s, it was not unusual for four generations to be living in one house. Farms were more like family compounds; simply surviving drought and famine was a team effort.

When Communism reorganized the country's economy and created the nonfilial "work unit," it was a labor change, but not necessarily an ideological one. Survival still depended on the collective success of your work unit, or *dan wei*.

The workforce became more mobile in the 1980s, but the *dan wei* is a large part of China's past, shaping its cultural philosophy. Urban housing is assigned by employers, making employees neighbors in their own apartment compound. It is not unusual for co-workers to date and then marry. The employer often provides childcare and recreation facilities as well. Consequently, many Chinese still live, work, and die within the same unit of friends and co-workers.

This partially explains the strong drive to save face. With your future entwined in a group, an affront to one family member or co-worker is an affront to everyone. This is even reflected in China's ancient religions, which preach a collective goal: a harmonious society (Confucianism) and harmony with one's surroundings (Taoism).

While the culture is atheistic, the Chinese way of living—with its emphasis on sharing, avoiding gluttony, responsibility for family, and being content with what one has (in general, putting others' needs above oneself)—seems inherently more "Christian," than the American lifestyle of *me, me, me*. In fact, you could argue that collectivism is often more of the biblical model than individualism.

Justus, the Tanzanian preacher, and his favorite verse flood back to my mind: "All the believers were united and shared everything. They would sell pieces of property and possessions and distribute the proceeds to everyone who needed them."[20] In the U.S., the verses we have engraved on coasters and refrigerator magnets are more like, "'I know the plans I have for you,' declares the Lord, 'plans to prosper you and not to harm you, plans to give you hope and a future.'"[21]

While the building blocks of Chinese culture are foreign to us, they are not foreign to God:

> *Blessed are the poor in spirit. Blessed are the meek.*

> *Blessed are those who are persecuted because of righteousness.*

> *Blessed are the Chinese, for theirs may be the kingdom of heaven.*

saluting your shorts

The Chinese equivalent of Mount Rushmore, the Dazu Rock Carvings in Sichuan province, contain more than 5,000 cliffside carvings depicting Buddhist, Confucian, and Daoist statues. Built as early as AD 650, they remain one of the ancient wonders of China—one of the few religious shrines to survive Mao's Cultural Revolution.

The culture is perhaps most deeply affected by Confucianism, but since this belief system does not honor any particular gods, it is not an official religion. Confucius believed that all men should be "gentlemen of good moral character," and that this was the key to an orderly society. Confucianism does not particularly address suffering, death, or the existence of a God.

Buddhism, by contrast, asserts that life is filled with suffering, and we can never be set free from pain as long as we are trapped in a cycle of reincarnation. Buddhism advocates separating oneself from worldly things and following "The Middle Way" (neither self-indulgence nor self-torture) to be liberated from this cycle and attain a state of peace and happiness, or *nirvana*.

If Confucianism is a guide to a moral society, and Buddhism offers relief from the pain of the human condition, Taoism urges a life close to nature—simple, uncomplicated, and free from excessive and unnatural responsibilities. Taoism incorporates numerous practices—like alchemy, astrology, martial arts, feng shui, and even cuisine to bring one's *qi* (personal energy) into harmony with *Tao*, the "path" or flow of the universe.

Thus on the next day, which is wet and rainy, Kyle and I visit a Buddhist temple. Our female taxi driver sings along to Chinese pop music on the radio, a Mao ornament swinging from the rearview mirror.

We walk up to the temple complex's inauspicious stone entrance. Once inside, a smiling woman greets us, handing us a thin stick. I look at Kyle curiously and he motions toward a small gathering of people burning incense in the stone courtyard. We walk around the back way by the monk dormitories. As we re-emerge toward the middle of the development, we hear chanting coming from a large room, doors and windows open. It is a dark room, lit by electric, red flower buds and a gold Buddha at the front. Winding solemnly in a snakelike formation are men and women dressed in brown robes, hands clasped, chanting slowly. The leader rings a tiny bell and everyone stops. The line eventually resumes, snaking its way around the room.

Kyle and I proceed to another large room with rows and rows of glass-enclosed statues. These are not statues of Buddha, I'm told, but statues of famous monks from this monastery through the centuries. For 10 RMB, a monk will come out, ask your age, match your age to an appropriate statue, and tell your fortune.

We move into another room with enclosed statues and a large, gold, laughing Buddha made into a shrine. A woman kneels on a round, yellow cushion, hands folded in prayer. To the left, we can see monks worshiping in a large, open-air room, shaved heads, some wearing brown, some black. Many who are dressed in gold robes with a red sash are kneeling on round, yellow cushions.

Finally, we pass the last courtyard containing a giant stone statue as tall as two houses. It is obviously used as a shrine, judging from the scattered flowers at its feet. Since the courtyard is deserted, I think about taking a photo, but before I can, an eager-looking Chinese man wearing a baseball cap taps us on the shoulder. He and his traveling companion are from a different region of China and would like their picture taken with *us*, the foreigners.

That evening, I go to dinner with Kyle and some of his friends, including Holly and Ben. We stop at a small convenience store on the way. Kyle heads to the back to get toilet paper, which is sold by individual roll under the brand name "Happiness." (I couldn't agree more.) I walk the aisles, trying to find anything with sugar. The Chinese aren't known for their desserts, and candy can be hard to find. I peek in the ice cream freezer to discover popsicles in the flavor of . . . corn and green pea.

As we walk back through the apartment complex to the main boulevard, I notice that laundry has appeared outside nearly every window. Shorts, pants, and shirts dangle precariously in the breeze—some as high as eight stories. It gives a whole new meaning to the phrase "airing dirty laundry." I pause to admire the solidarity of everyone's garments waving in the air like flags, marveling at the faith in one's neighbors not to steal them, and in the wind not to blow them halfway across town.

We stroll the winding streets, the mysterious seedy fluff still wafting through the air like snow, gathering in corners and gutters like fleece. Ever mischievous, Kyle has discovered that lighting the fluff with a lighter produces an instant burst of flame—burning brightly for a few seconds before fading away harmlessly.

We walk along, pretending we don't know Kyle, to a small restaurant in a neighboring plaza. I have always secretly wanted to eat nothing but steamed Chinese dumplings for dinner, and now I might get my chance. After we order our food, I watch a waitress pause at a neighboring table, holding two live chickens by the legs, apparently asking the couple which one they want.

The waitress soon brings us a massive order of dumplings, dumping them unceremoniously onto paper towels in the middle of the table. Nobody cares or bothers to ask for utensils as we dig in with our hands. As we eat, I ask Kyle's friends about some of the obstacles facing the church in China.

In China's eyes, there is no problem that government micromanagement can't solve, and Kyle's friends are quick to point out specific examples. When regional tobacco sales were flagging, the government ran a campaign encouraging people in Hubei province to smoke. In an attempt to stave off rain for the Beijing Olympics, atomizers were shot into the surrounding clouds (cloud seeding). In Shanghai, whether taxis have odd or even license plate numbers determines which days they may cross the river—the city's attempt to control traffic flow. To hide pollution, factories are often temporarily shut down preceding visits by international guests, says Ben.

Government debacles such as Tiananmen Square are removed from the history books and blocked from Internet search engines, along with international websites that have been known to contain less-than-flattering material about the government, such as CNN.com. YouTube, the Chinese Wikipedia, and Google are also blocked.

Back at Kyle's apartment, Kyle is having fun again setting the seeds on fire in the dark. It is Ben's birthday, and Holly has managed to save a box of cake mix from a care package and enough sugar to make homemade icing. When it comes out of the oven, she barely gets the frosting on before everyone literally pounces on it. Someone manages to find a knife to cut it with, but we six sugar-starved Westerners devour it straight from the pan.

I'm sure there's some kind of social commentary on the situation—how Americans are too dependent on sweets—but I am too busy stuffing my face with frosting to care.

silly string and spiced frog

On my last day in China, I am able to attend a Chinese wedding with Kyle. Two of his English-speaking Chinese friends have asked him to officiate the English part of their ceremony. A modern Chinese wedding is not as formal as a U.S. wedding—it's more like a game show, Kyle warns, looking over his script in the car. The couple is technically "married" weeks before after filling out all the government paperwork. The wedding/reception usually takes place at a nice restaurant and is more of a celebration than an actual ceremony.

The night before they are married, the groom and his buddies have a bachelor party that usually involves cards or poker and can last all night. They then drive in a procession to the bride's house. The groom walks up to the front door and loudly declares, "I am here to marry your daughter." The bride's family blocks the door and refuses to let him in, symbolizing their reluctance to give her up. They may also exchange red envelopes with money through the door.

This bride and groom have traditional Chinese names, but they are also known by their English names, Kitty and Clint. The restaurant's reception hall is filled with red, circular tables split by a long, red runway leading up to a white, heart-shaped arch. While waiting for the ceremony to start, I look at the bridal photos, which could best be classified as "senior portraits meets theme park." Along with Kitty in a traditional white wedding dress (rented for the occasion), are pictures of her and Clint on a carousel, posing with two fake giraffes, and with a cello.

As the ceremony starts, people clap and shout as the couple makes their way down the aisle, passing through the heart-shaped arch. Kitty wears a white strapless wedding dress with her hair piled high upon her head and a veil. Before the couple reaches the stage, a handful of guests pop out of the crowd and Silly-String them. I watch in horror—pink, lavender, and turquoise string dangling off the bride's perfectly coiffed head like squiggles of frosting—but Kitty laughs it off as if she were expecting this.

A spotlight appears to the right of the stage, and the mother of the groom speaks, then the father of the bride. The odd mix of background music includes "I Do Cherish You," "Turkey in the Straw," and Michael Buble's "Dance with Me." The spotlight shines on the couple, and Kyle is called to the stage to perform the English vows. For this special occasion, someone turns on a bubble machine. The non-English-speaking crowd talks among themselves as Kyle good-naturedly fends off bubbles with a wave of his script and motors quickly through the "I do's."

After a brief "You may kiss the bride," Kitty and Clint walk back down the aisle to greet their guests and pause for pictures. This is the servers' cue to begin the meal. The plates come fast and furious, placed on a spinning wheel in the center of the tables as everyone returns to their seats—pork balls, dumplings, pancakes, tofu, snail, shrimp, turtle, soup, spiced frog, fish balls, alpaca, clams, eel, and squirrel-fish.

The bride, who has changed into a red party dress, stops at each table to offer a traditional *baiju* toast with shot glasses. Depending on the number of tables, this requires a certain amount of stamina. As the guests converse, Kitty then joins her bridesmaids in the back of the reception hall to play "wedding games," more like what you would see at an American bachelorette party. This goes on for an hour or more as the guests finish eating. As we leave, we get a picture with Kitty, who has just finished eating a cucumber with two meatballs attached to it while being timed with a stopwatch.

That night, after the levity of the wedding, I think about all I have observed so far in China. The future of Christianity here is "nearly impossible to tell," says one of Kyle's friends. "Christianity changes so drastically from decade to decade."

When I think about China, I will remember tea, the crowded sidewalks, muggy heat, and lanterns with red tassels swinging from every store entrance. I also think about Kyle, setting seeds on fire in the gutter with a lighter.

Perhaps there is more to this than meets the eye.

Like the seeds—falling like fluff from the sky, blowing to and fro across China in the wind—all it takes to ignite the church is a small spark. Isolated on the concrete or in the gutter, the seeds produce only a small burst of flame before the fire dies out. Yet clumped together, they will burn for a while, providing a surprising flame for something so fragile.

To quote Brother Yun,

> I'm frequently asked why China is experiencing revival, but most places in the West are not. When I'm in the West, I see all the mighty church buildings and all the expensive equipment, plush carpets and state-of-the-art sound systems. I can assure the Western church with absolute certainty that you don't need any more church buildings. . . . When God moves in the West, it seems you want to stop and enjoy his presence and blessings too long, and build an altar to your experiences. . . . The first thing needed for revival to return to your churches is the Word of the Lord. . . .
>
> I pray that God might use the Chinese church to help the Western church rise up and walk in the power of the Holy Spirit.[22]

Amen.

Honduras

the banana republic

for the final step of my journey, I am meeting up with a twelve-member team from the U.S. to travel to Honduras, the original banana republic. We will spend a week with Honduran physician Dr. Jorge Ponce, doing medical missions in rural areas about an hour from the capital of Tegucigalpa.

Besides me, our group consists of cancer doctor Patrick Daugherty; nurses Charlotte and Melissa; Ron and Martha, retired lovebirds; Andrew and Christy, nursing students; and Ned, a retired motorcycle enthusiast; rounded out by twenty-somethings Emily, Jonah, Kayla, and Kristin.

At the airport, everyone waits, semi-stunned by the wee hours of the morning, for the airline desk to open. Ron looks like he is headed to war, wearing a camouflage backpack and red-white-and-blue striped suspenders. Andrew is full of energy as he plops down his luggage. "Should we start the revival now, or wait until we get on the plane?" he asks eagerly.

The airport in Tegucigalpa has one of the most dangerous commercial landings in the world. Pilots must bank in around a

range of mountains, then do a ninety-degree turn at a low alti-
tude before coming to a screeching stop on a six-thousand-foot
runway. Everyone is keenly aware of this as we start our descent.
When the plane slows to a crawl, everyone on board bursts into
applause. "Thank you!" the pilot responds from the cockpit.

"Oh look! Church's Chicken!" Christy calls from the seat behind me, pointing to a passing billboard.

There is something both comforting and revolting about
stepping outside the Honduran airport and seeing a Burger King,
Little Caesar's, Pizza Hut, and Baskin Robbins waiting to greet
you. Comforting because we know we won't starve, but revolting
because the first view of Tegucigalpa is lost behind a giant food
court.

We all pile into a van for the drive to Cofradia, which is just
over an hour away. The vistas beyond Tegucigalpa's congestion
are startlingly beautiful. Meanwhile, stacked houses—mostly
beige, with spots of peach and teal, roped off with sticks and
barbed wire—cover the hillside in what looks like the favelas of
Rio, with banana and mango trees all around.

Finally we arrive at "Camp Cofradia," a lovable but primitive
retreat center at the end of a pothole-riddled road. There are four
large buildings—one for church services, one soon to be used as
a nursing home, one dormitory, and one dining hall—their yards
dotted with roosters. I don't think the others appreciate yet what
it will mean to have roosters running around in the wee hours of
the morning.

Dinner is late, so we sit on the porch as rain starts to pepper
the roof and then begins gushing over the side of the building. A
Saturday night church service is underway in one of the nearby

buildings. Wailing and clapping drift through the building's open windows.

Someone asks, "Where's Andrew?"

"He and Jonah went up to the church service," Charlotte says.

Charlotte, with thirty years of teaching experience, is undeniably the veteran of the group, having been on more than twenty mission trips. Born and raised on the mission field in Nigeria, she returned to the U.S. for high school but always knew she wanted to be a nurse and longed to do missions once her kids were grown.

Emily, Kristin, and Melissa are also experienced travelers—Melissa has been to Honduras and Brazil, and Haiti earlier in the year to help with earthquake relief. Kristin, a recent graduate, has been to Europe with various mission teams. This is the first time abroad, however, for college students Kayla and Jonah.

"I spent last summer in Destin ministering to college students, and it changed my heart. I thought this trip would be a good opportunity to be with those who love and serve," Jonah says.

Kayla offers, "About a year ago, my home church asked if I would be willing to take over the kids' group. A month later, I started running the vans that pick them up. I have kids whose parents are incarcerated; one nine-year-old had been sold into prostitution for drugs. God completely used them to change my life. I really felt God calling me to work with kids on the mission field. I saw this as a way to get my feet wet."

A few minutes later, Andrew reappears, pushing hair back from his sweaty forehead "Whew! I can tell you one thing. If Western church services were like that, no one would be obese!"

The next day, Sunday, is quiet and cloudy. To my surprise, even the roosters seem to have slept in. Breakfast is Honduras's *plato tipico*, the local equivalent of the Denny's Sunrise Special—scrambled eggs, fried bananas, refried beans, sausage, and a tortilla. The electricity goes off promptly at 8:30. "The government turns it off during the day to conserve energy," someone explains.

We pile into a school bus and begin the descent into Tegucigalpa for church. The river is swollen with last night's rain and polluted with garbage. Finally we arrive at *Iglesia Amistad Cristiana* (Friendship Christian Church). Founded in 1986, IAC is nondenominational but would be considered Pentecostal in the States. The Tegucigalpa branch is the main church, with a little over two hundred members and six mission churches in the surrounding mountains.

Worship has already started when we arrive. The auditorium has a white-tiled floor with eight rotating fans spinning wildly. A twelve-member praise band and one of the pastor's daughters are leading worship. "He is here!" she shouts. "Thank you, Holy Spirit! Thank you, Jesus."

Our group is guided to the right of the stage, but I sneak up to the balcony to get a better view. The audience of one hundred or more is casually dressed, most in jeans. In time, the band, consisting of drums, a keyboard, and two guitars, picks up the tempo with a new song based on John 3:16. The chorus includes rowdy shouts of "Hey! Hey!" As the music crescendos, the audience starts to slip out of the rows and a group of men link arms and begin moshing in a circle. The music is deafening, the worship leader shouting, "We live for you, Jesus!"

One thing is for certain—it takes *stamina* to lead worship in Honduras. Some teenage girls soon form a mosh pit of their own. One man is dangerously close to knocking over a speaker near the stage. Andrew has figured out enough Spanish to pump his fist enthusiastically at the right time—"Hey! Hey!"

The balcony gradually starts to fill up with children. Soon one-third of the room is moshing, shirttails untucked. One woman is slain in the Spirit. The teenage girls form a conga line across the small auditorium. Now I understand why the children are in the balcony—so they won't get trampled. Someone else passes out in a chair, and Christy goes forward to see if anyone needs medical help.

Nearly an hour has passed and the worship continues. One young man who has been slain in the Spirit is in danger of getting trampled by oblivious dancers. A few of his friends approach to move his limp body. Ten minutes later, it looks like there has been a small skirmish—a handful of bodies littering the front of the church amid what could best be described as holy chaos. *Finally* the worship comes to an end. At the call for Sunday school, the children empty the balcony in a joyous stampede. Someone passes out water to the wilted Americans.

When we arrive back at the camp, we find the electricity again turned off, and no one is sure whether it will be back on tonight. In what seems to be another emerging pattern, the bottom falls out of the sky ten minutes later and it begins to *rain*. Dinner eventually turns out to be Honduran spaghetti with salsa mixed in, prepared with a kerosene stove. With the electricity off, we can't count pills for tomorrow's clinic like we had planned. Emily decides to brave a cold shower. She gathers her toiletries solemnly, as if marching to the foxholes instead of a grimy shower with a tattered dolphin curtain.

I settle in a chair beside Dr. Daugherty and Andrew on the porch. I ask Andrew what made him decide to make this return trip to Honduras.

"I just came to help people," he says simply. "At fifteen I started making selfish choices and it went on a long time without consequences. When I was about eighteen, the consequences started happening. At twenty-three, I just despised myself.

"I haven't been a Christian very long, but it's changing my life. When I started seeking a relationship with God, this opportunity came up and I said, 'That's me.'"

"And how does one of north Alabama's premier radiologists wind up in the mountains of Honduras?" I ask Dr. Daugherty.

"Well, growing up, I never planned to be a doctor," he says, leaning back in his chair. Born in the mountains of eastern Tennessee, his family was farmers, and they grew up poor, he says.

"I was the first one in my family to graduate from high school. I met my wife, Becky, my senior year. I was ready to get married when we graduated, but she had always wanted to be a nurse. I decided I would attend Lee College, flunk out, and then Becky and I could get married."

His college chemistry teacher, Mrs. Beech, saw something in him and turned him onto learning. "I went forty quarters without flunking a course and graduated. Becky and I married and moved into a trailer park.

"I didn't know anything about having a practice," he says. "The first years were very, very difficult. For three years, I was the only doctor in town, so I never turned my beeper off. I could never leave town."

Yet a strong desire to serve others kept him going, he says.

"My mom always said, 'Just look around; you'll find someone less fortunate than you.'"

Dr. Daugherty's words echo what I've heard from many others—that the path to the mission field isn't always linear, that God often reveals only one step of the plan at a time. The more I see of life, the more I think God tends to summon those who are *moving*—listening, but moving all the same.

The rain is now tapering off, and so has our conversation. All of a sudden, the electricity comes on with a crackling hum. Everyone cheers except for Emily, who has just finished an icy shower.

catrachos and gringos

In only a few days, I have learned there are eight "must knows" about Honduras:

The electricity comes and goes as it pleases.

Keep your mouth closed when you shower.

Don't flush the toilet paper.

Always trust a Honduran when they recommend you take the truck.

Keep a $20 bill in your sock at all times.

Don't take pictures of men with armed rifles. This is considered wildly inappropriate. (And even if it weren't, it's never a good idea to take secret pictures of men armed with rifles who don't speak the same language as you.)

Don't pat children on the head. They are adorable, and they may have lice.

Promise nothing. But still come through. If you even halfway imply that you might do something, you may as well have sworn on your life.

Breakfast the next morning is cereal and fruit. As we swap perspectives about yesterday's service, no one completely understands the phenomenon of being "slain in the Spirit," but no one passes judgment either.

"They appear to be *out* in a complete faint," Dr. Daugherty comments. "I've seen some people pass out and hit their heads on the floor to where they're bleeding. It doesn't look like just a swoon."

Andrew shrugs. "When the Spirit leaves the room, all you've got left is religion."

Everyone pauses. "What did you say?" asks Dr. Daugherty.

"When the Spirit leaves the room, all you've got left is religion," Andrew repeats.

No one really knows what to say. We just know something profound has been dropped in the middle of our cereal.

Half an hour later, we all climb in the bus for our first medical clinic. It is at least an hour to the mountain town of Talanga. The children there stare at us soberly as we pull in. The local term for Hondurans is *catrachos*, and the term for Americans ("white foreigners") is *gringos*. A bus full of Americans is apparently the morning's entertainment.

Outside the church, eighty to ninety people are already waiting. They burst into applause when we enter the courtyard, a humbling experience for someone like me with no medical training.

The church is a twenty-by-thirty-foot one-room building. Jonah, Ned, Ron, and I claim a quarter of it for the pharmacy table and start filling plastic bags with the specified doses, while nurse Melissa hands out prescriptions and dosing instructions. Kayla, Martha, and Andrew are working one triage table, getting vital signs and symptoms, while Emily and Kristin work another. Several of the youth at the church serve as translators, including Dr. Ponce's son Bryan, who attends a bilingual school.

Once the patients have their checkup paperwork, they proceed to one of the three tables manned by Dr. Daugherty, Charlotte, Dr. Ponce, and Christy.

A small boy sits intrepidly at Charlotte's table. She asks where the pain is, and he nervously recites his full name instead. His mother says he is here for stomach problems, congestion, and cough. His sister has a visibly bloated stomach with worms. "*Dolor de gargantua* [sore throat]?" Christy asks a five-year-old girl.

Charlotte is examining a woman with four children. She turns to the youngest son, Jeffrey, who is complaining of ear/nose/throat symptoms and diarrhea.

"Diarrhea" means stomach worms 95 percent of the time, and it is one of the most common complaints. The water is full of parasites, Dr. Daugherty explains, and unless a patient has been previously treated, everyone is given worm medicine. Tylenol, Ibuprofen, Benadryl, and Robitussin are also fast leaving our pharmacy.

Christy examines the throat of a seven-year-old girl whose swollen tonsils are almost touching. "She would have been scheduled for surgery if she were in the U.S.," she says.

At the pharmacy table Jonah is hurriedly bagging orders for Melissa, while Ron and Willie count out multivitamins. The children watch longingly; most have never seen pills before and think they're candy.

Andrew and Martha's table might as well be the torture table, considering how the children scream at the sight of a stethoscope and digital thermometer wielded by the foreigners.

When the clinic halts for lunch, I join Dr. Ponce at one of the tables and ask him to tell me his story. "I was saved in 1985," he says. "I only went to church for one year, and then fell away from the Lord.

"My life was a disaster," he confesses. "I had problems with alcohol." One time, when his oldest son , Bryan, was two, Dr. Ponce says he drank twelve beers in one day. Then Bryan came to him and said, "Daddy, give me some beer!"

"I felt like there was a knife inside my heart," the doctor recalls. "I heard a voice say, 'Look what you are doing to my son.'"

He pauses. "I thought I was crazy, hearing voices. Then the voice told me again, 'Look what you are doing to your son.' I threw the beer away."

He adds, "My financial situation at the time was really, really bad. But when I reconciled with the Lord, God started teaching me the best way to do things."

Dr. Ponce says he used to complain about the trials of having a practice until "one day when I was making house calls, they didn't have anything to eat in the first house. I saw only tortillas, and they were so hard. Eleven people were living there, and they were smiling. And the Holy Spirit spoke to my heart, 'See those people? They don't have anything compared to you, and they are happy.' I asked forgiveness from the Lord and I told him, 'I won't complain anymore. I will start working for your kingdom.'

"I don't have my own practice now," he tells me. "And we don't charge, even in church, with a program that feeds 250 children twice a week. God provides the medicine, even my support and salary."

One of the things Dr. Ponce has learned in making his rounds is that people need education, not just medical treatment. "If we don't teach them how to prevent disease, we aren't doing anything valuable."

When lunch is over, we resume with the afternoon crowd.

Charlotte examines a one-year-old girl and her mother. "How many days has she been throwing up?"

"Your stomach hurts? Where does it hurt? Here? Here?"

Kayla scrambles to write down the symptoms of a grandmother with high blood pressure. Christy is tending a girl with a painful burn on her thumb. The girl winces as she swabs it with iodine.

"The reason he's not eating may be because of the worms," Dr. Daugherty tells one mother, raising his voice over the noise.

"We don't have heartburn medicine for someone that young."

"Crush the multivitamin and give it to her."

"Is there anyone in your family who hasn't been treated that we need to send worm medicine home for?"

"When you get home, boil some water. When it cools, fill this prescription bottle up to the line."

Ron is throwing candy out the window, to squeals of delight. As for me, I think I'll be handing out Benadryl and counting pills in my sleep.

We pack up to leave in the early afternoon. "How many patients did we see?" someone asks Melissa.

"I don't know . . . three hundred?"

We all plop down in the bus, slightly dazed.

"I think Andrew is in his element," Dr. Daugherty says with a smile. A few seconds later, Andrew bounds on the bus. He surveys our tired group. "Looks like children of the Most High God to me!" he exclaims before sliding into a seat.

spreading the blessing

besides coffee, my favorite beverage would have to be Diet SunDrop. For those of you who have never had Diet SunDrop, it's similar to Diet Mountain Dew, but more awesome.

Growing up, you knew you had officially come of age in the Hudson house when Mom let you drink SunDrop at the dinner table. The first time I realized our family's addiction to SunDrop was the summer I was seventeen, when we decided to take a two-week vacation out West in the family van. The challenge came when it was time to stock up on SunDrop. SunDrop is regional—available in Tennessee and parts of Alabama, but only randomly found west of the Mississippi. We were going where no Hudson had gone before—into states unreached by SunDrop.

Once my dad had sufficiently obtained a "three-week" supply of canned drinks and loaded it with the luggage, he realized the SunDrop was stacked too high to see out the back of the van. Thus, my sister and I were tasked with breaking down the flats and storing the individual cans throughout the van—in pouches, under seats, even under the bag in the trashcan. For years afterward, if you opened some seldom-used compartment, you ran the risk of a stray SunDrop rolling out and hitting you in the head.

Anyway, I don't know if it was being stuck in the car for twenty-two hours, or if the arid desert climate made us more thirsty than anticipated, but despite my dad's best calculations, we were running out of Diet SunDrop only ten days into our journey, somewhere around Moab, Utah.

My dad was the first to pick up on the scarcity and began rationing (aka hiding) cans from the last flat. My mom then bought cans of Diet Mountain Dew at some desert outpost, which sat in the backseat of the car like an unwanted stepchild. Despite admonitions to alternate beverages, we quietly depleted the precious stash of Diet SunDrop. My mom got suspicious when my dad volunteered to climb over us children to get her a drink while she was driving. She *really* got suspicious when he offered to pour it in a cup of ice instead of simply tossing her the can.

"This isn't Diet SunDrop!!"

"I don't know what you mean."

"How many SunDrops have you had today?"

"Two, but I didn't have *any* yesterday!"

"You had one back at Canyonlands—I saw you!"

The drama rose to such heights that a child was dispatched to watch the parent pouring the drink at all times to verify that it was, in fact, Diet SunDrop.

Children can be easily bribed with small amounts of chocolate.

Anyway, the moral of the story is: my parents knew what they wanted and would accept no imitations. They knew the taste of their beloved SunDrop well enough to be able to spot a fake without having to check the can.

I think back to the worship services in Honduras and Brazil—the energy and enthusiasm that exuded into the rafters. If we don't settle for imitations with our soft drinks, why do we sometimes settle for a watered-down walk with God?

When the Spirit leaves the room, all you've got left is religion.

The following day, by 9:00 a.m., fifty people are lined up outside our camp, waiting to be seen. By 9:15, the line has doubled. Today the patients move through so rapidly, Melissa gets backed up twenty deep in the pharmacy, and Dr. Ponce comes over to help. Dr. Daugherty examines a little girl with curly hair and a cough who won't eat. She has a dark purple rash on her chin; the milk from the mangoes irritates and burns the skin, her mother says. He calls Dr. Ponce over, who says it's a parasite.

Ron is trying to rig up a curtain so women can have breast exams without Charlotte having to troop down to the bunkhouses. In between patients, Bryan and Dr. Daugherty are having a contest to see who can kill the most flies. Charlotte is now looking at a rash on the leg of a twenty-month-old who cut himself on a can. Andrew is straining to hear the heartbeat of a screaming child. Christy chastises a man in his fifties with high blood pressure and a long history of smoking. "*No fumar*!"

"We're seeing a lot of fungus and nonproductive cough," Dr. Daugherty notes. "The greatest thing that can be done here to improve the quality of life is clean water."

By the end of the week, the group is starting to sag a little. Two members of the group are having stomach trouble; Christy has a migraine, and Kayla has lost her voice. We awaken on Friday to our last day of clinics. At breakfast, Dr. Ponce's son Bryan is wearing Honduran blue. Honduras is playing in the World Cup, he explains, and Fridays are National Pride Day. Bryan moves between the tables, translating. Whenever anyone threatens to flag in the heat, Bryan cheerfully reminds them of why we're here: "spreading the blessing."

We get ready for the drive to Casa Quemada. "These people have never had a clinic before," Dr. Ponce explains.

Instead of our normal bus, there are pickup trucks to meet us because the roads are so rough. With eighteen people and only room for two or three in each truck cab, that means some of us are riding in the back. Melissa, Kristin, Kayla, the pastor's daughter, Millie, and I climb into the bed of the red truck. To make more room, Melissa and Kristin sit on the sides, gripping two iron bars on the cab.

"You know this would be illegal in the U.S," I say to Millie as we lurch forward.

"The police here will only pull you over if you have more than four or six people," she replies.

I watch the guys' truck bump down the driveway crammed with ten people, and possibly some more I can't see stuffed down in the truck bed. *Great, so we're illegal even by Honduran standards*, I think.

Whether it's relief that we don't go overboard with the first few potholes, or the thrill of doing something we've been forbidden to do since we were kids, the forty-five-minute drive passes quickly.

We unload at Casa Quemada Mission Church and quickly set up tables and chairs.

Dr. Daugherty starts by examining Carol, seven, who has a headache and swollen lymph nodes. Christy's first patient is a toothless grandmother with brown, wrinkled skin. "Someone fell on her during a church service," Bryan explains. Normally this would lead to further questioning, but after witnessing Sunday's services, no explanation is needed.

Charlotte is examining a grandmother with three youngsters in tow. Andrew and Martha are monitoring the blood pressure of a woman in her fifties.

Kristin is taking the temperature of an old woman and her three-year-old grandson, who walks with a slight spraddle. Emily hands him a green lollipop, and he looks at her uncertainly. The grandmother has stomach cramps and sore throat. "His blood pressure is a little high. Does he have pain in his ear?" Dr. Daugherty shouts above the din.

Young Bryan is blowing up latex gloves into balloons while Ron, Ned, and Jonah handle prescriptions. We are out of Tylenol before lunch. Kayla jots down triage info for a mother with four squirming children under six. Ned chases a few stray dogs out of the clinic.

By 3:00, the sweat is pouring. "Think of all the money people pay in the U.S. to go to a sauna," Dr. Daugherty says, wiping his face.

On the return ride, I sit next to Melissa and Ron.

"The people are the reason I keep coming back," says Ron. "We're here for a short period of time, but they live here every day. They're so far behind in their living standards. But they don't complain."

I think about the Hondurans, who have no dental care, no eye care, and no oncology. "If you get cancer, you live with it," Dr. Daugherty remarks grimly.

As for childbirth, "the majority of the ladies in the mountains use a midwife," says Dr. Ponce, though "one lady at the church delivered her own babies alone in the grass."

Yet Honduras is home to more than four thousand unemployed doctors who lack the means to practice, says Dr. Ponce. "It's the system . . . the corruption here in the government." I ask him what he thinks of the U.S. After a pause, he says, "Well, you have everything there."

Dr. Ponce says when visiting the states, he was particularly taken aback by the waste of food. "My wife—she was shocked."

He also noticed how busy things are.

"Life is so different," he says.

As the trucks navigate potholes, I think about how, too many times, we in the U.S. are content to live happily within our box.

Somewhere along the dusty roads of Tegucigalpa, I decide I will stop living inside the box.

make a run for the border

That evening I sit on the front porch with a Styrofoam cup of coffee, listening to the rain splash off the roof. Getting coffee in the evening has been difficult, as the power often goes out without warning. The coffee in Honduras is strong and natural, taken without artificial sweeteners or flavors.

I think about how different this is from Brazil, where the coffee is polluted with sweetener, and Wales, where the coffee is weak like the tea. I think of the red, homegrown beans in Tanzania, where commercialism hasn't quite set in and if you want coffee, you pretty much have to plant it yourself; and China, where the national drink is tea—steeped in tradition and uniformity.

Honduras, by contrast, is fertile soil for delicious and inexpensive coffee—bold and earthy, with no pretenses. In the biblical parable of the sower, if the U.S. is the seed getting choked out, Britain the seed falling on hard soil, and China the seed being snatched by birds, then Honduras would be the seed falling on fertile soil—an unassuming people, simple in lifestyle.

Getting ready soon to head back to America—home of mo-
chachinos, frappachinos and grande caramel lattes—I'm not sure
how I feel about the land of supersized sanctuaries, amusement
park-style VBSs, and praise band worship with multicolored
spotlights.

I'm finding I sort of like my coffee black.

On our last day in Honduras, we load our luggage before traveling to Tegucigalpa National Park, where we will stop on our
way to the airport.

About twenty minutes into our travels we encounter a bridge
submersed under a foot of rushing water, thanks to the overnight
rains. Dr. Ponce claims it's safe to proceed, but everyone else is
nervous. Ultimately the decision is made to let the truck with the
luggage go first. If the luggage makes it across safely, the people
will follow.

Somehow, this is not very comforting.

The luggage survives without incident, and everyone tries to
look calm when our turn comes. We cross with the van's sliding
door open, just in case.

Forty-five minutes later, we arrive at the national park and are
soon standing atop a small mountain. Dr. Daugherty, Andrew,
and I climb a nearby replica of Mayan ruins. Then we walk to an
enormous statue of Christ overlooking the park and capital.

As we bid Honduras farewell, the three of us take pictures
under the statue with the colorful cityscape behind us. Unlike
the Corcovado, who looks like he's about to dive off the cliff, this

Christ has his hands lowered and extended, as if opening his arms to a beloved child. Andrew is unusually quiet and thoughtful.

"Look, Andrew," says Dr. Daugherty, motioning toward the statue. "What do you see? A God who is yelling at you, or one who is welcoming you home?"

We stand there for a moment in solitude, thinking on these words. Then we head down the hillside, below the Christ, with his arms outstretched for us all.

Since my journey began under a statue of the Christ, I suppose it is fitting that it should end here as well. On the flight to the U.S., I reflect on my personal journey.

When I was growing up, I didn't want to hear the word *no*.

"Will you play with me?"

"Can I spend the night with Jana?"

"Can I have another cookie?"

"Can I stay up late?"

No, no, no and no.

I remember running down the hall and into my parents' bedroom with my latest request, holding my breath and hoping I didn't get the dreaded response.

When I got older, I realized, of course, that there are reasons parents say no . . . and reasons God says no. Still, I remember that same feeling of asking God for something when I was a teenager, and holding my breath with anticipation, hoping he didn't turn me down.

As an adult, I am convinced that one of God's most overlooked kindnesses is the beauty of no. It usually takes hindsight to realize this, of course. Looking back, I am thankful for a few key moments in my life when I asked God for something and he gently said no. Sometimes not so gently.

As a result, I am not really afraid of *no* anymore. That doesn't mean I'm not *disappointed* when I pray diligently for something and don't get it. But I feel secure enough now in God's character to generally not be terrified when he tells me no.

I wish the opposite were true—that I could say the same about *yes*.

Yes leads to a whole series of events; not *no*.

No is safe. *Yes* is not.

I used to think *no* was the worst answer you could get. But now I find my questions to God are changing.

Do I need to give more?

Are you calling me to the mission field?

If I gave my life to you, would you rewrite it?

And therein lies the shift.

I used to be afraid of *no*. Now I think I am afraid of *yes*.

It only took traveling to five countries to realize this.

If I had to condense what I have learned in the past few months to five thoughts, it would be this:

The spirit world is active (Brazil).

It doesn't take theology to drive believers from Christ, just apathy (Britain).

The issue of sharing faith in Third World countries is as complex as offering aid and financial assistance (Tanzania).

The most atheistic country in the world is also, surprisingly, the most ripe for spiritual harvest (China).

And, you haven't seen raw church until you've worshiped with Latin Americans (Honduras).

Once you've lived a little outside the box, how can you go back to it? There are lessons to be learned about faith, the prosperity gospel, persecution, and religious fervor—all adding different flavors when mixed with the church. Many blends, but one church. And one Father of us all.

If God called you to cross borders, would you do it?

I don't just mean geographically. We all have our own borders, whether they're denominational, national, or even self-imposed fear.

I think sometimes God beckons us to cross borders, not because he wants us to live there but because he wants to broaden our sights. I can't tell you what borders you should cross or when you should cross them. Only that Christianity isn't a box with rigid sides . . . it is a moving, flowing thing.

From the sweeping view of the Corcovado, I could understand the church as a city on a hill. In Revelation, John writes of a holy city that does not need the sun or moon to shine on it, because the Lord gives it light and the Lamb is the city's lamp—the nations will walk by its light.[23]

As the church, we all depend on this light. And on earth, we rely on other believers more than we know. What I mean is, the body of believers around the world keeps the church from being one-dimensional, one American blend.

And yet, when we look around the Lord's throne one day at the nations assembled there, I think we will actually be fascinated by what we all had in common. We all chose, despite earthly persecutions or American doubts, to believe in a God who, in many ways, remains a deep mystery. Those who lived where the church was diluted chose to seek out a pure stream. Those who lived where Christ was continually choked out chose to search for him amid the clutter and noise. Those who lived where the message was scarce chose to find it. Those who lived surrounded by the gospel chose to go where it was not.

We all depended on a pursuit of God, and we will stand before the throne on that day because we answered the invitation. We trusted in prayer. We leaned on each other's fellowship. We bet our lives on Scripture, and offered worship to an unseen deity.

We will find on that day that we all depended on coffee, tea . . .

And of course, holy water.

about the author

Amanda Hudson is a writer and Alabama native living in
Nashville, Tennessee. A graduate of Auburn University,
Hudson has written for numerous publications, including
Southern Living, *mental_floss* magazine, Purepolitics.com,
Motivation Strategies magazine, *The TimesDaily,* and *The Auburn
Plainsman*. In her spare time, she enjoys photography, coffee,
travel, and Auburn football.

For more information on any of the outreaches mentioned in
Coffee, Tea, and Holy Water,
please visit:
www.coffeeteaholywater.com

acknowledgments

Special thanks to: Debra Simmons, Global Missions of Mercy, Bryan and Jannet Carruth, Adam Copeland, Jody Gamble, David and Karen Morgan, Drs. Danny and Nancy Smelser, Linda Zelnik, Molly Goen, Jeremy Painter, Richard and Ann Bathew, Sarah Kharbuli and Parmarsan Thangkhiew, Dr. Jorge Ponce, Dr. Patrick Daugherty, Dr. Anthony Saway, Andrew Kallemeyn, Kenneth Purdom, Lauren Jacobs, and Keith and Carolyn Hudson.

appendix

Author's note: Below are some condensed advice and travel tips:

Just Go

I'm often asked for advice related to international travel and mission work. My main advice is just go. Is this your first mission/ humanitarian trip? If so, *just go.* Don't overthink it. Go with a group and get your feet wet.

How Can I Help?

If you've been on more than one mission or humanitarian outreach, it's great to keep going, but start asking yourself more targeted questions:

- Is there a particular organization I am interested in?

- Is there an area that appeals to me most?

- Do I like working with kids or adults? Medical mission trip/building trip/VBS?

- Is this an effort I can support long-term?

It's important not to do a hit-and-run. Once you've gotten your feet wet, plug in to a need or cause you feel passionate about. Try to avoid poverty tourism.

Am I Called to Missions?

YES. Your life is a mission, whether you travel internationally or not. You don't have to travel twelve hours on a plane to discover needs inside or outside your comfort zone.

Everyone needs a little *Coffee, Tea, and Holy Water.* Find yours and take it to the people outside your box.

Resources for International Travel:
- U.S. State Department: http://travel.state.gov/content/passports/english/go/checklist.html

- Center for Disease Control: http://wwwnc.cdc.gov/travel/notices/

- U.S. Customs and Border Protection: http://www.cbp.gov/travel/international-visitors/kbyg/international-travel-tips

- TravelZoo: http://www.travelzoo.com/from-the-deal-experts/20-tips-before-traveling-internationally/

- Travel and Leisure: http://www.travelandleisure.com/travel-blog/carry-on/2014/2/18/12-tips-to-make-international-travel-easier

Author's Travel Tips:
- Buy a travel guide and research where you're going before you go, even if there are limited opportunities for tourism. The guide will help you understand and appreciate more of what you see.

- Be advised, certain vaccinations such as hepatitis A and B, meningitis, tetanus, and typhoid, as well as malaria medication (oral) are not needed for tourism but are often required for humanitarian work in Third World countries. Check with your group leader or the Center for Disease Control (CDC) website.

- Pay close attention to airline bag weight requirements for carry-ons and checked bags. Note that this can vary by five to ten pounds at a moments' notice with changes in international requirements, so be flexible. Due to space, you may not actually be able to "carry on" your carry-on, even if it meets U.S. requirements, so be prepared with a smaller purse or bag.

- Keep all prescriptions and valuables (cameras, electronics, etc.) on you, in your carry-on, and not in your checked luggage.

- Be sure and check out what the weather is actually like during the dates you'll be visiting a particular area—not the average highs and lows depicted in the travel guide.

- Prepare for two extremes anyway—bring at least one or two outfits for tropical temperatures and one or two outfits (layers) for colder temperatures, regardless of where you're going. You never know what the temperature will be like at night, or when you'll get caught on a mountaintop with no jacket.

- Be aware of "rainy" seasons. If your destination has a rainy season that lasts two or three months, be prepared for rain for a few hours every day. This can affect everything from clothes to shoes and hairstyle choices.

- Look up the local currency/exchange rate to get an idea of how far your money will go. Inquire as to whether your projected destination takes debit/credit cards at most stores and restaurants or whether cash is the primary mode of operation.

- Photocopy important documents (passport, debit/credit cards, etc.) before going. Buy a luggage lock, and keep backup documents locked in your suitcase at all times. If a passport is lost or stolen, it will help tremendously to have a photocopy.

- Keep everything important (passport, etc.) *on you* at all times using a money belt under your clothes, unless you are engaging in activities that would jeopardize their safety. Having your passport and/or money locked in your suitcase in the room is of no use when your suitcase gets lost or stolen.

- Bring bug spray, sunscreen, anti-diarrheal medicine, and an extra roll or two of toilet paper, regardless of where you're going. Plan to use flip-flops in the shower, even if it is a hotel room.

- After leaving your home country, be wary of foreign ice and water. Stick only to bottled water and canned or bottled drinks, even if it is a western restaurant or chain, to be safe.

- Plan on the unexpected/delays. Depending on your destination, be advised that travel delays, cancellations, and vehicle breakdowns, as well as unexpected store and commercial closures can and will happen. Keep a fluid schedule and budget an extra day or so into your schedule to accommodate the unexpected.

- Be sensitive about taking photos. In some cultures, including many Third World countries, taking pictures of strangers is a sensitive and sometimes even an economic or religious issue.

- When traveling internationally, there's a good chance you will need an inexpensive plug adaptor for the local outlets. These are generally sorted by regions—North America/Europe/Asia, etc. Having a plug adaptor does *not* convert the voltage, however—and there can be a big difference in the electrical current. Check the voltage requirements for your area of travel and see whether a voltage convertor or actual transformer is needed for key appliances. This is especially key with appliances requiring a lot of voltage, such as hair dryers, or sensitive electronics, such as computers and phones.

Good luck!
Mandy

notes

1. Matthew 11:28-29.

2. 2 Samuel 6:21-22 NIV.

3. *Merriam Webster Dictionary.* Merriam-Webster.com 2012.

4. John 3:8.

5. John 3:11.

6. C. S. Lewis, *The Screwtape Letters* (San Francisco: HarperCollins, 1996), 123, 46, 57.

7. C. S. Lewis, *The Problem of Pain.* (San Francisco: HarperCollins, 1996).

8. Rick Warren, *The Purpose Driven Life* (Grand Rapids: Zondervan, 2004), 173.

9. Job 1:9-11.

10. Job 38:3-4.

11. Job 40:8.

12. Selections from Job 38.

13. Dylan Thomas, "Do Not Go Gentle into That Good Night," Academy of American Poets, Poets.org. 2012.

14. Francis Chan, *Crazy Love* (Colorado Springs: David C. Cook, 2008), 21–22.

15. C. S. Lewis, *The Screwtape Letters* (San Franscisco: HarperCollins, 1996), 60–61.

16. All safari quotes taken from Alexis C. Kelley, Fodor's *The Complete African Safari Planner* (New York: Random House, 2008), 46–47, 49.

17. 1 Peter 4:10.

18. Paul Hattaway and Brother Yun, *The Heavenly Man* (Grand Rapids: Monarch Books, 2002). 54.

19. Randy Alcorn, *Safely Home* (Wheaton, IL: Tyndale House, 2001), 109.

20. Acts 2:44-45.

21. Jeremiah 29:11 NIV.

22. Hattaway and Yun, *The Heavenly Man*, 295–96.

23. Revelation 21:23.

bibliography

"2001 Census (England and Wales)." The Office for National Statistics, U.K. http://www.ons.gov.uk/ons/guide-method/census/census-2001/index.html.

Alpha News no. 44. U.K. Edition. (July–October 2008).

BBC News. "'One in 10' Attends Church Weekly." April 3, 2007. Accessed October 22, 2009, http://news.bbc.co.uk/2/hi/uk_news/6520463.stm.

BBC News. "UK among Most Secular Nations." February 26, 2004. Accessed October 22, 2009, http://news.bbc.co.uk/2/hi/programmes/wtwtgod/3518375.stm.

Eyewitness Travel Guides: China. New York: D.K. Publishing, 2005.

Fry, Plantangenet Somerset. *Best Castles.* Cincinnati: David and Charles Limited, 2006.

Great Britain. Lonely Planet. Oakland, CA: Lonely Planet Publications, 2007.

Honduras and the Bay Islands. Lonely Planet, edited by Greg Benchwick. Oakland, CA: Lonely Planet Publications, 2009.

Insight Guides: Brazil. New York: Langenscheidt Publishers, 2008.

Insight Guides: England. New York: Langenscheidt Publishers, 2008.

Jenkyns, Richard. *Westminster Abbey.* London: Profile Books, 2004.

Kardec, Allan. "Spiritism Easily Explained." (Based on the essay "O Espiritismo em sua mais simples expressão" by Allan Kardec, 2nd ed. FEESP 1989.) www.ssbaltimore.org/resources/SEE.pdf.

Kardec, Allan. Spiritist Society of Baltimore (SSB). e-Books. 2007.

Lowry, Lois. *The Giver.* New York: Dell Laurel-Leaf, 1993.

McLlwain, John. *Westminster Abbey.* Pitkin Guides. Andover: Pitkin Unichrome, 1999.

Mojo, Dambisa. *Dead Aid.* New York: Farrar, Straus and Giroux, 2009.

Viva: Together for Children. na.viva.org.

Westminster Abbey. Norwich, England: Jarrold Publishing, 1999.